COOKING WITH

Chef Jade

THE ULTIMATE **VEGAN & VEGETARIAN** COOKBOOK

Jadeandzelda.com

Paperback: 978-1-312-07264-0
Ebook: 979-8-218-28778-8

First paperback edition October 2023.

Printed by LuLu Press, Inc. in the USA.

FOREWORD

When my sister, Jade, told me she was writing a cookbook, I said, "It's about time."

You know those little kids that have one thousand plastic pots and pans from ten different kitchen sets littered around the house? That was my sister. Those kids that always want to "help" in the kitchen? Jade. The kids that always looked at the food menu before the rides at the State Fair? You get the idea.

Jade has so much passion for cooking (and eating) that I always knew she was destined to do big things. I watched as the little girl who made dinner with our mom every night grew up to become the woman who has now eaten her way across the globe in a bold exploration of her roots. I mean, ever since she began sharing her recipes, experiences, and travel revelations on her blog, www.cookingwithjade.com, in 2020, she has inspired others to eat outside the box. A cookbook was the obvious next step.

But, truthfully, my sister started this journey long before her blog or this book. You see, when you're adopted, you spend a lot of time thinking about your biological background, something Jade and I have always bonded over as adoptees. Forever in search of her ethnic roots and in love with the world, my sister was born a traveler at heart. After culinary school, she backpacked around the world, learning not only about the cultures she came from but everything she could about, literally everything.

This book is equal parts food and culture, with little bits of info about where each dish comes from sprinkled in. In that way, this cookbook is so much more than recipes: it's a pocket shrine to the world.

In these pages, you'll find my sister's soul expressed in a loving rainbow of vegan/vegetarian dishes. You'll also find some of my favorite things to eat, familiar flavors I grew up on, and the recipes that I remember when my best friend is halfway across the world and I miss her. You'll find the best of Jade's experiences, her life and all the people that have touched it, some of the tastiest cultures around the world, and the unconditional love our adopted parents raised us with.... you'll also find some top-notch food to share with your special people.

As you read this book, keep your heart open, your mind curious, your skin cleansed, and your stomach full.

With love and gratitude,

Naveen

THE WORK OF A (PARTIAL) LIFETIME

Well, it's finally happened…I've written a cookbook. If you had "Chef Jade Cookbook" on your bingo card, you can cross it off now (you'll have to keep waiting for my set of custom potholders). I've collected a lot of amazing recipes during my travels across the globe—some of which I have been privileged to share with you on my site, www.cookingwithjade.com. But I wanted to put my all-time favorites in print because A) I'm a hopeless book lover, B) I know some of you still prefer to read your recipes that way, and C) this was an easy way to get into your home and become a part of your family. 😊

This cookbook, like my blog, has been an incredible journey. I got into this itinerant cooking gig as a way to connect with my multicultural roots, and researching this cookbook has deepened those connections. Each of these recipes holds meaning for me. You'll find recipes from my formative trip to Japan, where I had the joy of exploring my biological mother's homeland. You'll find recipes that explore my biological father's Jamaican roots. And you'll find plenty of recipes from my adopted homeland—no less meaningful for their familiarity.

I've also had the privilege of visiting my ancestors' homelands: places like Italy, China, and Mexico. And so many other amazing destinations. I took those trips to learn more about food – yes – but also about the cultures that produced them. And I hope to impart some of that knowledge through this cookbook. That's why I have added short blurbs about each country represented. I hope that this cookbook is more than just a collection of recipes: I hope it's an homage to the places those recipes came from.

But of course, no cookbook is worth its Himalayan rock salt if the food itself isn't tasty. And I am here to tell you that these recipes are downright delicious. These are the dishes that I turn to time and time again in my own kitchen, the meals that my foodie friends keep asking for more of. You'll find dishes for every meal and occasion, and I hope you find at least a few recipes that will become permanent fixtures in your repertoire.
Sorry, all this talk of food is making me hungry.

Let's start cooking, shall we?

♡,

Chef Jade

TABLE OF CONTENTS

1

INTRODUCTION

2

RECIPES

3

VEGAN PANCAKES

Did you know that pancakes were invented by the ancient Greeks, way back in 600 BCE? While Americans didn't invent this hearty breakfast dish, we've sure made it our own: we consume roughly 700,000 flapjacks each year! We even have a "National Pancake Day" in February. When that day rolls around, whip up some delicious vegan pancakes using this simple recipe. On second thought, might as well whip them up this morning....you know you're craving them.

PREPARATION TIME
10 MINUTES

COOKING TIME
20 MINUTES

SERVES
8 PANCAKES

INGREDIENTS

- 1 1/2 cup flour
- 1 tbsp baking powder
- Pinch of salt
- 2 tbsp sugar, maple syrup, or agave
- 1 cup oat milk
- 1/2 cup water
- 2 tbsp oil

DIRECTIONS

1. In a large bowl, whisk together the flour, baking powder, salt, sugar, maple syrup, or agave.
2. Add the oat milk, water, and oil to the dry mixture.
3. Stir the mixture using a large spoon until just combined. Don't worry about a few lumps; overmixing can make the pancakes dense.
4. Heat a large griddle or pan over medium-high heat.
5. Grease the heated pan with a small amount of vegan butter or coconut oil.
6. Drop about 1/3 cup of pancake batter onto the pan for each pancake.
7. Cook the pancakes until you see bubbles forming on the surface.
8. Carefully flip the pancakes and cook for an additional minute on the other side.
9. Once cooked, remove the pancakes from the pan and repeat the process with the remaining batter.
10. Add your favorite toppings, like blueberries, raspberries, or syrup!

BAGELS

Confession time: I wasn't a huge bagel person until I moved to New York. These crusty breakfast staples - brought over by immigrants from Eastern Europe - are as much a part of New Yorkers' hectic mornings as crowded subway rides. The standard bagel is inherently vegan, primarily consisting of water, flour, yeast, and salt (there's beauty in simplicity). I've added a few small adornments, but at just six ingredients, this is a simple recipe that carries on the classic bagel tradition.

PREPARATION TIME
15 MINUTES (PLUS RISING TIME)

COOKING TIME
50 MINUTES

SERVES
8 BAGELS

INGREDIENTS

- 1 packet (2 1/4 tsp) active dry yeast
- 1 1/2 cups warm water (about 110°F or 45°C)
- 1 tbsp sugar
- 3 1/2 cups all-purpose flour (plus extra for kneading)
- 1 tsp salt

- 1 tbsp vegetable oil (plus extra for greasing)
- 1 tbsp maple syrup or agave syrup (for boiling)
- Toppings of your choice: sesame seeds, poppy seeds, minced onion, minced garlic, etc.

DIRECTIONS

1. In a small bowl, combine the warm water, sugar, and yeast. Let it sit for about 5-10 minutes or until the mixture becomes frothy and bubbly.
2. In a large mixing bowl, combine the flour and salt. Make a well in the center and pour in the yeast mixture and vegetable oil.
3. Mix the ingredients until a dough forms. Turn the dough out onto a floured surface and knead for about 5-7 minutes until the dough is smooth and elastic. Add more flour if needed to prevent sticking.
4. Shape the dough into a ball and place it in a lightly greased bowl. Cover the bowl with a damp cloth or plastic wrap and let the dough rise in a warm place for about 1 hour or until it has doubled in size.
5. Preheat the oven to 425°F (220°C) and line a baking sheet with parchment paper.
6. Punch down the risen dough to deflate it. Turn it out onto a floured surface and divide it into 8 equal portions.
7. Roll each portion into a ball and use your thumb to make a hole in the center. Gently stretch and shape the hole to form a bagel shape.
8. Place the shaped bagels onto the prepared baking sheet and cover them with a clean cloth. Let them rest for about 10-15 minutes.
9. While the bagels are resting, bring a large pot of water to a boil. Stir in the maple syrup or agave syrup.
10. Carefully lower the bagels into the boiling water, a few at a time. Boil for about 1-2 minutes on each side. This step gives the bagels their characteristic chewy texture.
11. Remove the boiled bagels from the water using a slotted spoon and place them back on the baking sheet.
12. If desired, sprinkle your choice of toppings over the bagels while they are still wet.
13. Bake the bagels in the preheated oven for about 15-20 minutes or until they are golden brown.
14. Remove the bagels from the oven and let them cool on a wire rack before slicing and serving.
15. Enjoy your freshly baked vegan bagels with your favorite spreads or toppings!

FRITTATA

The frittata is like the omelet's more festive, more forgiving cousin: it's easier to cook and *hot take* more fun to eat. Though it was invented in Naples, Italy ("frittata" derives from the Italian word for "fried"), it has certainly held its place in American breakfast culture. The deep skillet allows you to throw in a whole mess of tasty ingredients. With eggs, this is a filling, nutritious vegetarian breakfast. By substituting tofu for the eggs, you can make it fully vegan. The latter has been one of my breakfast standbys for years.

PREPARATION TIME
15 MINUTES

COOKING TIME
25 MINUTES

SERVES
4 SERVINGS

INGREDIENTS

- 8 large eggs
- 1/2 cup milk or non-dairy milk (e.g., almond milk, soy milk)
- 1 tbsp olive oil
- 1 small onion, diced
- 1 bell pepper, diced
- 1 cup baby spinach or chopped spinach
- 1 cup cherry tomatoes, halved
- 1/2 cup grated cheese (e.g., cheddar, mozzarella, or non-dairy cheese)
- Salt and pepper, to taste
- Fresh herbs (such as parsley or chives), for garnish

DIRECTIONS

1. Preheat your oven's broiler.
2. In a bowl, whisk together the eggs and milk. Season with a pinch of salt and pepper. Set aside.
3. Heat the olive oil in a large oven-safe skillet over medium heat.
4. Add the diced onion and bell pepper to the skillet. Sauté for about 3-4 minutes or until the vegetables are softened.
5. Add the baby spinach to the skillet and cook for an additional 1-2 minutes until it wilts.
6. Pour the egg mixture into the skillet over the sautéed vegetables.
7. Arrange the halved cherry tomatoes on top of the egg mixture.
8. Sprinkle the grated cheese evenly over the top.
9. Cook the frittata on the stovetop for about 5-6 minutes, or until the edges are set, but the center is still slightly runny.
10. Transfer the skillet to the preheated broiler and broil for about 3-4 minutes, or until the top is golden brown and the center is fully set.
11. Remove the skillet from the oven (remember that the handle will be hot!) and let the frittata cool slightly.
12. Carefully slide a spatula around the edges of the frittata to loosen it from the skillet.
13. Slice the frittata into wedges and serve.
14. Garnish with fresh herbs, if desired.
15. Enjoy your delicious vegetarian frittata as a breakfast, brunch, or lunch option!

AVOCADO TOAST

As an aspiring social media maven, I have to admit I'm a little jealous of avocado toast. This dish is a social media superstar. In fact, it become so trendy that it's almost a punchline these days, which is a shame because it really is an incredible dish. It's tasty, healthy, and easy to make—exactly what I look for in a quick breakfast. And when you make it yourself, it's actually quite affordable. Seriously, I can't tell you how many dollars this avocado toast recipe has saved me. More money to explore the world with!

PREPARATION TIME
15 MINUTES

COOKING TIME
NO COOKING REQUIRED

SERVES
4-6 PEOPLE

INGREDIENTS

- 3 avocados

TIP: Make sure to squeeze the avocado a bit to ensure it is slightly squishy. Too firm and it's not quite ready.

- 1/4 tsp salt
- 1 pinch pepper
- 1 sweet onion
- 1 garlic clove
- 1 pinch of smoked paprika (optional)

DIRECTIONS

1. Dice the sweet onion and mince the garlic.
2. In a medium-sized bowl, peel, pit, and mash all three avocados until you achieve a desired consistency.
3. Add the diced sweet onion, minced garlic, 1/4 tsp of salt, a pinch of pepper, and a pinch of smoked paprika (if using) to the mashed avocados.
4. Mix all the ingredients together until well combined.
5. Ideally, serve the avocado dip with rosemary sourdough bread or rye bread.

SMOOTHIE BOWL

I know that a few of my followers read my vegan recipes for health reasons. Well, this recipe is for you (slash anyone looking for a fresh, flavorful breakfast). It's packed with nutrients and features some superfoods like kale, kiwi, and banana. Plus, it's downright creative and fun, if I do say so myself. I mean, how often do you get to eat a smoothie out of a bowl? With this recipe, as much as you'd like.

PREPARATION TIME
15 MINUTES

COOKING TIME
NO COOKING REQUIRED

SERVES
2 SERVINGS

INGREDIENTS

Base:
- Kale
- Almond milk
- Banana
- Avocado
- Ice
- Honey

Toppings:
- Banana
- Kiwi
- Mango
- Chia Seeds
- Drizzled agave

DIRECTIONS

1. Wash and remove the tough stems from the kale leaves. Tear the leaves into smaller pieces.
2. In a blender, combine a handful of kale leaves with:
   - 1 ripe banana
   - 1/2 avocado (peeled and pitted)
   - A handful of ice cubes
   - 1 cup of almond milk
   - 1-2 tbsp of honey (adjust to taste)
3. Blend the ingredients until you achieve a smooth and creamy consistency. If the mixture is too thick, you can add more almond milk to reach your desired consistency.
4. Taste the smoothie and adjust the sweetness or thickness by adding more honey or almond milk if needed.
5. Once the smoothie is blended to your liking, pour it into bowls.
6. For the toppings, dice:
   - 1 banana
   - 1 kiwi
   - 1/2 mango
7. Sprinkle chia seeds over the smoothie.
8. Top the smoothie with the diced banana, kiwi, and mango.
9. Drizzle a small amount of agave over the top for added sweetness.
10. Serve the kale smoothie immediately and enjoy!

CHICKPEA SALAD

Chickpeas are a staple in the Middle East, and I enjoyed many delicious preparations during my travels there (especially hummus, which I still dream about from time to time, but I digress). This unique recipe makes chickpeas the star of a fresh, filling salad. It's a Mediterranean-inspired dish that can be made even more Mediterranean with the addition of optional ingredients like olives, feta (or vegan feta), and mint. While light and lemony, this salad packs some protein from the chickpeas and could serve as a healthy meal. Since I've been known to eat my weight in chickpeas, this is a recipe I turn to pretty often.

PREPARATION TIME
15 MINUTES

COOKING TIME
NONE

SERVES
4 SERVINGS

INGREDIENTS

For the Salad:
- 2 cans (15 ounces each) chickpeas, drained and rinsed
- 1 cucumber, diced
- 1 red bell pepper, diced
- 1/2 red onion, finely chopped
- 1 cup cherry tomatoes, halved
- 1/4 cup fresh parsley, chopped

For the Lemon Dressing:
- 1/4 cup fresh lemon juice (approximately 2 lemons)
- 1/4 cup extra-virgin olive oil
- 2 cloves garlic, minced
- 1 tsp Dijon mustard
- 1 tsp agave syrup or maple syrup
- Salt and pepper to taste

DIRECTIONS

1. In a small bowl, whisk together the fresh lemon juice, extra-virgin olive oil, minced garlic, Dijon mustard, agave syrup, salt, and pepper. Set the dressing aside.
2. In a large mixing bowl, combine the drained and rinsed chickpeas, diced cucumber, diced red bell pepper, finely chopped red onion, cherry tomatoes, and chopped fresh parsley. If you're adding optional ingredients like olives, vegan feta cheese, or fresh mint leaves, add them to the bowl as well.
3. Pour the lemon dressing over the salad ingredients in the bowl.
4. Gently toss all the ingredients together until they are well coated with the lemon dressing. Be careful not to mash the chickpeas while mixing.
5. Refrigerate the salad for at least 30 minutes before serving to allow the flavors to meld together. You can also let it chill longer if you prefer a colder salad.
6. Before serving, give the salad a final toss to redistribute the dressing. Garnish with extra parsley or mint leaves if desired.

STUFFED BELL PEPPERS

Growing up, bell peppers stuffed with ground beef and cheese were a staple at our house. It's one of those comfort foods I really started to miss when I went vegan. Luckily, I've got this recipe to see me through those extra nostalgic days. Heads up: this recipe isn't fully vegan since it calls for cheese, but you could hold the dairy for a truly vegan meal. It may not be exactly like home, but believe me, it's close enough.

PREPARATION TIME
20 MINUTES

COOKING TIME
40 MINUTES

SERVES
4 SERVINGS

INGREDIENTS

- 4 large bell peppers (any color), tops removed and seeds removed
- 1 cup cooked quinoa or rice
- 1 can (15 oz) black beans, drained and rinsed
- 1 cup corn kernels (fresh, frozen, or canned)
- 1 cup diced tomatoes (canned or fresh)

- 1/2 cup diced onion
- 1/2 cup shredded cheese (cheddar, mozzarella, or vegan cheese)
- 1 tsp ground cumin
- 1 tsp chili powder
- 1/2 tsp garlic powder
- Salt and pepper, to taste
- Olive oil, for drizzling

DIRECTIONS

1. Preheat your oven to 375°F (190°C).
2. Prepare the bell peppers by cutting off the tops and removing the seeds. Rinse them thoroughly.
3. In a large mixing bowl, combine the cooked quinoa or rice, black beans, corn kernels, diced tomatoes, diced onion, shredded cheese, ground cumin, chili powder, garlic powder, salt, and pepper. Mix well to combine all the ingredients.
4. Stuff the mixture into the hollowed-out bell peppers, pressing down gently to fill them evenly.
5. Place the stuffed bell peppers in a baking dish that's been lightly greased or lined with parchment paper.
6. Drizzle a bit of olive oil over the tops of the stuffed peppers to help them cook and brown in the oven.
7. Cover the baking dish with aluminum foil and place it in the preheated oven.
8. Bake the stuffed bell peppers for about 25-30 minutes, or until the peppers are tender and the filling is heated through.
9. Remove the foil and continue to bake for an additional 5-10 minutes, or until the cheese on top is melted and bubbly and the tops of the peppers are slightly browned.
10. Carefully remove the stuffed bell peppers from the oven.
11. Allow the stuffed bell peppers to cool slightly before serving.
12. Serve the vegetarian stuffed bell peppers on a plate and enjoy your hearty and flavorful meal!

ROASTED BUTTERNUT SQUASH SOUP

To me, butternut squash soup is the ultimate fall comfort food (and I do love fall). Eating it always reminds me of my weekend trips to New England during peak foliage season. So when fall arrives, grab your cardigan, enjoy that pumpkin spice latte you've been craving all year, and heat up a pot of this delicious butternut squash soup. And maybe invite me over while you're at it? I'll bring the pumpkin ale.

PREPARATION TIME
50 MINUTES

COOKING TIME
10 MINUTES

SERVES
3-4 SERVINGS

INGREDIENTS

- 2 butternut squash
- 2 tbsp olive oil, divided
- 1 cup diced onion
- 1/3 cup honey
- 1/3 cup pine nuts, lightly toasted
- 1 tbsp minced garlic
- 1 1/2 tsp ground sage
- 1 1/2 tsp ground cumin
- 2 cups vegetable stock
- 5 cups water
- 1/4 tsp roasted ground ginger
- 1/2 tsp sea salt
- 1/2 tsp ground black pepper

DIRECTIONS

1. Preheat the oven to 400°F (200°C). Cut the squash in half lengthwise and remove the seeds. Brush with 1 tbsp of olive oil.
2. Place on a baking sheet and roast for 35-45 minutes or until tender. Remove the pulp from the squash in a bowl and set aside.
3. In large saucepan over medium-high heat, add olive oil and onion; sauté for 3 minutes. Add the squash and the rest of the ingredients, except the pine nuts. Bring to a boil and then simmer for about 15 minutes.
4. Remove from fire.
5. In a blender or food processor puree your ingredients.
6. To serve, garnish with pine nuts.
7. Serve and enjoy!

BUFFALO WINGS

While the origins of many classic dishes are a little murky, buffalo wings have a very distinct provenance. They were invented at the Anchor Bar in - you guessed it - Buffalo, NY in 1964. As the story goes, owner Teressa Bellissimo was working the kitchen late one night when her son and his friends came in wanting a snack. Not having much on hand, she fried some chicken wings and tossed them in hot sauce. The rest is history. Today, Americans consume over a billion Buffalo wings on Super Bowl Sunday alone! But Buffalo still does them best. This recipe takes the best flavor profiles of the various vegan wings I ate in Buffalo. They're sure to be a hit at your next Super Bowl Party.

PREPARATION TIME
15 MINUTES

COOKING TIME
25 MINUTES

SERVES
4 SERVINGS

INGREDIENTS

- 1 large head of cauliflower, cut into florets
- 1 cup all-purpose flour or chickpea flour (for gluten-free)
- 1 cup non-dairy milk (e.g., almond milk, soy milk)
- 1 tsp garlic powder
- 1 tsp onion powder
- 1/2 tsp smoked paprika
- 1/4 tsp salt
- 1/4 tsp black pepper
- 1 cup vegan buffalo sauce (store-bought or homemade)
- 2 tbsp vegan butter, melted
- Celery sticks and vegan ranch or blue cheese dressing, for serving (optional)

DIRECTIONS

1. Preheat your oven to 450°F (230°C). Line a baking sheet with parchment paper.
2. In a large mixing bowl, whisk together the flour, non-dairy milk, garlic powder, onion powder, smoked paprika, salt, and black pepper to make the batter.
3. Dip each cauliflower floret into the batter, making sure it's evenly coated, and shake off any excess batter.
4. Place the coated cauliflower florets on the prepared baking sheet in a single layer, leaving some space between them.
5. Bake the cauliflower in the preheated oven for about 20-25 minutes, or until the florets are crispy and golden brown. You can flip them halfway through baking for even cooking.
6. In a separate mixing bowl, whisk together the vegan buffalo sauce and melted vegan butter.
7. Once the cauliflower is baked, carefully transfer the hot florets to the bowl with the buffalo sauce mixture. Gently toss the florets to coat them evenly with the sauce.
8. Return the coated cauliflower florets to the baking sheet and bake for an additional 5-10 minutes to help the sauce adhere and caramelize slightly.
9. Remove the buffalo cauliflower wings from the oven and let them cool slightly before serving.
10. Serve the vegan buffalo cauliflower wings with celery sticks and vegan ranch or blue cheese dressing, if desired.
11. Enjoy your delicious and spicy vegan buffalo wings alternative!

CREAM OF MUSHROOM SOUP

This is another comfort food that I simply can't get enough of. Nothing warms the soul quite like a good bowl of cream of mushroom soup. Of course, it also works wonders as a binding agent in other recipes. That's how it earned the nickname "America's bechamel." Eating it always takes me back to the potlucks and get-togethers of my Midwestern youth. And if you've only had the canned variety, this version will blow you away. Trust me, your casserole game will reach a whole new level.

VEGETARIAN

PREPARATION TIME
20 MINUTES

COOKING TIME
25 MINUTES

SERVES
4 SERVINGS

INGREDIENTS

- 2 tbsp butter
- 1 lb of fresh mixed mushrooms (slice)
- 1/2 tsp salt
- 1/4 tsp pepper
- 1/3 chopped onion
- 1/4 cup of flour
- 1 can of vegetable broth
- 1/4 cup chives
- 3 garlic cloves
- 1 pinch smoked paprika (optional)
- 1/2 cup of cream

DIRECTIONS

1. In a large saucepan, heat butter over medium-high heat; saute mushrooms, chives, garlic, and onions until tender.
2. Mix flour, salt, pepper, and 1 can broth until smooth; stir into mushroom mixture.
3. Stir in the remaining can of broth. Bring to a boil; cook and stir until thickened, about 2 minutes.
4. Reduce heat; stir in cream. Simmer, uncovered, until flavors are blended, about 15 minutes, stirring occasionally.
5. Add smoked paprika for garnish and taste.

STUFFED SPAGHETTI SQUASH

What we call "spaghetti squash" actually originated in China, entering the historical record in the mid-nineteenth century. This particular variety of winter squash got its name because - when cooked - its thin strands of flesh resemble spaghetti. In fact, it's often used as a vegan substitute for noodles. With this recipe, though, we'll be stuffing it–creating a colorful, filling meal that is sure to be a hit at home. No bowls required.

100% VEGAN

PREPARATION TIME
10 MINUTES

COOKING TIME
15 MINUTES

SERVES
4 SERVINGS

INGREDIENTS

- 1 spaghetti squash, halved and seeded
- 2 cups of tomato sauce
- 5 button mushrooms cut into pieces
- 1 tbsp extra virgin olive oil
- 4 tbsp basil (fresh or frozen)
- 1 pinch of salt
- 1 pinch of pepper

DIRECTIONS

1. Preheat the oven to 180°C (360°F).
2. Place the spaghetti squash halves cut side down on a baking sheet.
3. Bake for 40 minutes or until flesh is tender.
4. With a fork, scrape the flesh to obtain the spaghetti texture.
5. Add a drizzle of olive oil, salt and pepper.
6. Divide half of the tomato sauce, mushrooms, cheese and basil into each squash half and mix.
7. Bake again for 15 minutes. Serve immediately and enjoy!

CHILI

When I think chili, I think of Texas, one of our country's great food states. And one that always adds a few inches to my waistline; as they say, everything's bigger in Texas. If you ask most Texans, they'll tell you that a good bowl of chili should have lots of ground beef and no beans! This being a vegetarian-friendly cookbook, I've 86'd the beef and added a heap of red beans. Sorry, Texas. I'd like to think that after a spoonful of this rich, flavorful chili, all will be forgiven.

100% VEGAN

PREPARATION TIME
10 MINUTES

COOKING TIME
45 MINUTES

SERVES
4 SERVINGS

INGREDIENTS

- 1 pound of peeled tomatoes
- 1 pound of tinned cooked red beans
- 1 ½ cups of button mushrooms
- 2 handfuls of textured soy protein
- 1 onion
- 1 clove of garlic
- ½ tsp of cumin powder
- ½ tsp of oregano powder
- 2 tbsp of olive oil
- 1 pinch of salt
- 1 pinch of ground black pepper

DIRECTIONS

1. Peel and mince the onion and garlic. Drain the red beans.
2. Clean and slice the button mushrooms into strips.
3. Chop your vegetables, and then carve an onion.
4. Heat 2 tbsp of olive oil in a casserole dish. Sauté the onion and the garlic until they become translucent. Add drained kidney beans and textured soy protein and cook for 5 minutes, mixing well.
5. Add the peeled tomatoes, the mushrooms then the cumin, and the oregano. Add salt and pepper. Simmer over low heat for about 45 minutes, stirring regularly. Add water if needed.
6. Serve hot with white rice.

MAC AND CHEESE

This is another one that takes me back to childhood. In fact, I suspect that if you were to ask our youngest foodies what their favorite food was, mac & cheese would land pretty high on the list. It's simple, it's cheesy (always a plus with kids), and it's packed with flavor. And while it originated in Northern Europe, Americans of all ages have made it their own. Whether you're cooking for your kids or are a kid at heart, this recipe is sure to please. And with a few extra touches like paprika, garlic, and olive oil, it offers plenty for the grown-up palate as well.

PREPARATION TIME
50 MINUTES

COOKING TIME
15 MINUTES

SERVES
3-4 SERVINGS

INGREDIENTS

- 1 lb of elbow pasta
- 1/2 cup of unsalted butter (or vegan butter)
- 1 lb of cheddar cheese (or vegan cheese)
- 1 medium onion
- 1 clove of garlic
- ¼ tsp paprika
- ½ tsp of salt
- Pinches of pepper
- 1 tbsp of olive oil

DIRECTIONS

1. Boil the elbow pasta until it's tender to your liking. Drain and then set aside.
2. Saute the onion and garlic together until the onions are translucent. Try not to burn the garlic.
3. Combine pasta, garlic, onions, paprika, salt, and pepper. Now, layer the pasta into a baking dish.
4. Shred the cheddar cheese and set aside.
5. Layer pasta and evenly place quarter-size butter cuts on top of the layer. Now sprinkle the shredded cheese on the layer, making sure to cover the pasta completely.
6. If you have enough pasta for another layer, then repeat the above step.
7. Place in oven at 350° for 20-30 minutes. You are waiting for the cheese to melt completely and get to your desired brownness.
8. Serve and enjoy your dish!

VEGETARIAN BURGER

Is there a more "American" food than the classic burger? Maybe apple pie, but let's be honest, which do we eat more of? The hamburger as we know and love it is believed to have originated at a classic New Haven, CT eatery called Louis' Lunch (New Haven also boasts its own delicious style of pizza–not bad for a small New England town!). They still steam the burger and serve it on sliced bread, as they've been doing for over a hundred years. Unfortunately, they don't offer veggie burgers, but I've got your back. This vegetarian burger recipe with cashew cheese brings a big burger flavor without the beef. Add toppings to your taste; I'm a pickle, onion, ketchup, and mustard girl myself.

PREPARATION TIME
15 MINUTES

COOKING TIME
15 MINUTES

SERVES
4 SERVINGS

INGREDIENTS

For the Patties:
- 2 cups cooked and drained black beans (canned or cooked from dried)
- 1/2 cup breadcrumbs
- 1/4 cup finely chopped onion
- 1/4 cup finely chopped bell pepper (any color)
- 2 cloves garlic, minced
- 1 tsp cumin powder
- 1 tsp paprika
- 1/2 tsp salt
- 1/4 tsp black pepper
- 1 egg (or flax egg for vegan option)
- 2 tbsp olive oil (for cooking)

For Assembling:
- 4 whole wheat burger buns
- 4 slices cheddar cheese (or vegan cheese)
- Lettuce leaves
- Sliced tomatoes
- Sliced red onion
- Pickles
- Ketchup and mustard (optional)

DIRECTIONS

1. In a large mixing bowl, mash the black beans using a fork or potato masher until mostly smooth but with some texture remaining.
2. Add breadcrumbs, chopped onion, chopped bell pepper, minced garlic, cumin powder, paprika, salt, black pepper, and egg (or flax egg). Mix well until all ingredients are combined.
3. Divide the mixture into 4 equal portions. Shape each portion into a patty, making sure they are firm and hold together well.
4. Heat olive oil in a skillet over medium heat.
5. Once the skillet is hot, add the patties and cook for about 4-5 minutes on each side or until they are golden brown and cooked through.
6. In the last minute of cooking, place a slice of cheddar cheese on top of each patty and cover the skillet with a lid to allow the cheese to melt.
7. While the patties are cooking, prepare your burger buns by toasting them lightly in a toaster or on a grill.
8. To assemble the burgers, place lettuce leaves on the bottom half of each bun, followed by a cooked patty with melted cheese.
9. Top the patties with sliced tomatoes, red onion, and pickles.
10. Add ketchup and mustard if desired.
11. Place the top half of the bun on each burger to complete the assembly.
12. Serve your delicious vegetarian cheeseburgers with your favorite side dishes, and enjoy!

VEGETARIAN ZUCCHINI GRATIN

As you may have guessed, potatoes au gratin (that is, browned and sprinkled with cheese and breadcrumbs) originated in France. More specifically, it originated in Southeastern France in the late 18th century. But Americans have since made it their own, and the dish has become a potluck favorite. For a healthier - but still tasty - version, I'm substituting the potatoes with sliced zucchini. This easy-to-make dish is sure to be a hit at your next get-together.

PREPARATION TIME
15 MINUTES

COOKING TIME
15 MINUTES

SERVES
4 SERVINGS

INGREDIENTS

- 2 tbsp unsalted butter
- 3 pieces zucchini, peeled, halved, seeded, and cut into 2- x 1/2-inch strips (4 cups)
- 1/8 tsp sugar
- 1/4 cup chopped fresh chives
- 2 tsp chopped fresh tarragon
- 1 tsp coarsely chopped fresh dill
- 1 tsp lemon zest, grated
- 1/3 cup breadcrumbs
- 1/4 cup grated parmesan cheese
- ¾ tbsp salt
- Black pepper

DIRECTIONS

1. Preheat the oven to 375°F. Add butter in a saucepan over medium heat until it's melted. Cook for 3 minutes, or until beginning to brown.
2. Toss sliced zucchini in a rectangular cake pan with 1 tbsp brown butter, salt, and sugar. Bake for about 25 minutes.
3. Remove the dish from the oven, and preheat the broiler. Add chives, tarragon, dill, and lemon zest to zucchini, and toss to coat. Season with pepper, if desired.
4. Stir together breadcrumbs, parmesan, and remaining 1 tbsp brown butter in a bowl. Sprinkle breadcrumb mixture over zucchini. Broil for 2 minutes, or until crumbs are golden brown.
5. Serve and enjoy!

TOMATO SOUP AND GRILLED CHEESE

As I said earlier, kids love a cheesy meal, and grilled cheese and tomato soup are the only classic childhood dish that gives mac & cheese a run for its money. This soul-warming dish was one of my favorites growing up: a lunch I always looked forward to. Like my mac & cheese, this recipe is a little different than what you probably ate as a kid. I've added red pepper for the perfect touch of heat and a little basil for contrast. That might sound slightly more sophisticated, but don't worry: this is still childhood comfort in a bowl.

PREPARATION TIME
15 MINUTES

COOKING TIME
25 MINUTES

SERVES
3 SERVINGS

INGREDIENTS

Grilled Cheese:
- 6 slices of your favorite bread (whole wheat, sourdough, etc.)
- 1 1/2 cups grated cheddar cheese (or any cheese of your choice)
- 1/2 cup sliced tomatoes
- 1/4 cup finely chopped red onion
- 1/4 cup sliced black olives
- 2 tbsp butter or margarine
- 1 tsp olive oil
- Salt and pepper to taste

Tomato and Pepper Soup:
- 1 red pepper
- 1 cup of tomato juice
- 1 shallot
- 1 clove of garlic
- 1 small can of tomato puree
- 2 tbsp of cream
- 1 pinch of salt
- 1 pinch of ground black pepper
- 1 cup of chopped basil
- 1 cup of pine nuts
- 2 tbsp of olive oil

DIRECTIONS

1. Sauté the minced shallot, the minced garlic clove, and the red pepper cut into thin strips in olive oil for 10 minutes.
2. Pour in the tomato juice and leave to simmer for 10 minutes.
3. While simmering the soup, start by preparing the filling for your grilled cheese sandwiches. In a bowl, combine the grated cheddar cheese, sliced tomatoes, chopped red onion, and sliced black olives. Mix them together to create a flavorful and colorful filling.
4. Lay out 3 slices of bread on a clean surface. Divide the cheese and veggie filling equally among the 3 slices, spreading it evenly.
5. Place the remaining 3 slices of bread on top of the filling to create sandwiches.
6. In a skillet or griddle, heat half of the butter (1 tbsp) and olive oil over medium heat.
7. Once the butter is melted and the skillet is heated, carefully place the sandwiches in the skillet. Cook for about 3-4 minutes on each side or until the bread is golden brown and the cheese is melted. You can press the sandwiches down gently with a spatula to help the cheese melt.
8. While the sandwiches are cooking, you can spread a bit of butter on the top side of each sandwich.
9. Once both sides are golden brown and the cheese is melted, remove the sandwiches from the skillet.
10. Allow the sandwiches to cool for a minute before cutting them in half.
11. Add the tomato puree and the cream to the simmering soup. Mix everything.
12. Season with 1 pinch of salt and pepper; then dry toast the pine nuts. Gently place them on the soup; then sprinkle with basil.
13. Pair your sandwich and soup for a comforting meal!

CORN CHOWDER

Growing up in rural Illinois, summer was always corn season. We would buy it at a roadside stand and eat it just about any way we could: cornbread, corn pudding, and corn on the cob. Corn chowder was one of my favorites, though - especially as we started to approach fall. I love a warm, hearty soup; this corn chowder will always be close to my heart. A spoonful takes me back to those carefree late summer days in the Prairie State. And I'd love for you to come with me.

PREPARATION TIME
15 MINUTES

COOKING TIME
25 MINUTES

SERVES
4 SERVINGS

INGREDIENTS

- 2 tbsp olive oil
- 1 medium onion, chopped
- 2 cloves garlic, minced
- 3 medium potatoes, peeled and diced
- 4 cups fresh or frozen corn kernels
- 4 cups vegetable broth

- 1 cup unsweetened almond milk (or any plant-based milk)
- 1 tsp dried thyme
- 1/2 tsp smoked paprika
- 1/4 tsp turmeric (optional, for color)
- Salt and pepper to taste
- Chopped fresh parsley or chives (for garnish)

DIRECTIONS

1. In a large pot, heat the olive oil over medium heat. Add the chopped onion and sauté for about 3-4 minutes until it becomes translucent.
2. Add the minced garlic and sauté for an additional 1 minute, until fragrant.
3. Add the diced potatoes to the pot and stir well to combine with the onions and garlic.
4. Pour in the vegetable broth and bring the mixture to a boil. Reduce the heat to medium-low, cover the pot, and let the potatoes simmer for about 10-15 minutes or until they are tender.
5. Remove about 1 cup of the cooked potatoes and broth from the pot and set it aside.
6. Blend the remaining mixture in the pot until smooth and creamy using an immersion or a regular blender.
7. Return the reserved potatoes and broth to the pot, along with the corn kernels, dried thyme, smoked paprika, and turmeric (if using). Stir to combine.
8. Pour in the unsweetened almond milk (or other plant-based milk) and stir again. Simmer the chowder for an additional 5-10 minutes to heat the corn and allow the flavors to meld.
9. Season the chowder with salt and pepper to taste. Adjust the seasoning as needed.
10. Serve the vegan corn chowder hot, garnished with chopped fresh parsley or chives.
11. Enjoy your creamy, flavorful vegan corn chowder as a comforting and hearty meal!

CHOCOLATE CHIP COOKIES

I've made and eaten countless desserts in my time, but chocolate chip cookies will always be the dessert I crave the most. Chocolate chip cookies were invented in the 1930s at the Toll House Restaurant in Whitman, MA, where owner Ruth Wakefield broke off chunks of a Nestle semi-sweet chocolate bar and baked them into her cookies. American servicemen from Massachusetts helped spread the chocolate cookie's popularity during World War II, sharing the delicious cookies they received in their care packages with their fellow troops (I don't know if I could have done the same, tbh). I thought my chocolate chip cookie days were over once I went vegan, but this recipe captures the magic of those first warm, gooey bites.

PREPARATION TIME
15 MINUTES

COOKING TIME
10-12 MINUTES PER BATCH

SERVES
24 COOKIES

INGREDIENTS

- 1 cup unsalted butter, softened (or use vegan butter for a dairy-free option)
- 3/4 cup granulated sugar
- 3/4 cup packed brown sugar
- 2 large eggs
- 1 tsp vanilla extract
- 2 1/4 cups all-purpose flour
- 1 tsp baking soda
- 1/2 tsp salt
- 2 cups chocolate chips (semi-sweet or dark chocolate)

DIRECTIONS

1. Preheat your oven to 375°F (190°C). Line a baking sheet with parchment paper.
2. In a large mixing bowl, cream together the softened butter, granulated sugar, and packed brown sugar until the mixture is light and fluffy.
3. Add the eggs, one at a time, beating well after each addition. Stir in the vanilla extract.
4. In a separate bowl, whisk together the all-purpose flour, baking soda, and salt.
5. Gradually add the dry ingredient mixture to the wet ingredients, mixing until just combined.
6. Fold in the chocolate chips until they are evenly distributed throughout the cookie dough.
7. Drop rounded tablespoons of cookie dough onto the prepared baking sheet, leaving some space between each cookie.
8. Bake the cookies in the preheated oven for about 10-12 minutes or until the edges are golden brown and the centers are slightly soft.
9. Remove the baking sheet from the oven and let the cookies cool on the sheet for a few minutes before transferring them to a wire rack to cool completely.
10. Repeat the baking process with the remaining cookie dough if needed.
11. Once the cookies are completely cooled, store them in an airtight container.
12. Enjoy your delicious vegetarian chocolate chip cookies with a glass of milk or your favorite beverage!

LEMON BARS

Here's a day you never knew existed: October 15th, National Lemon Bar Day. Normally, I would laugh at such a specific holiday, except I love lemon bars. And I know how I'm celebrating next time October 15th approaches: by busting out this recipe and whipping up a batch of sweet, tart lemon bars. These lemon bars are bright and zesty, just the way I like them. In fact, why wait till October? I have some baking to do.

100% VEGAN

PREPARATION TIME
20 MINUTES

COOKING TIME
45 MINUTES

SERVES
16 BARS

INGREDIENTS

For the Crust:
- 1 cup all-purpose flour
- 1/4 cup powdered sugar
- 1/2 cup vegan butter, softened

- Powdered sugar, for dusting

For the Lemon Filling:
- 1 1/4 cups granulated sugar
- 1/4 cup cornstarch
- 1/4 tsp salt
- 1 cup lemon juice (about 4-5 lemons)
- Zest of 2 lemons
- 1 cup non-dairy milk (e.g., almond milk, soy milk)
- 1/2 tsp turmeric (for color, optional)

DIRECTIONS

1. Preheat your oven to 350°F (175°C). Grease a 9x9-inch baking pan or line it with parchment paper for easy removal.
2. Crust: In a bowl, combine the all-purpose flour, powdered sugar, and softened vegan butter. Mix until the ingredients come together and form a crumbly dough.
3. Press the crust mixture evenly into the bottom of the prepared baking pan.
4. Bake the crust in the preheated oven for about 15-20 minutes or until it's lightly golden around the edges. Remove from the oven and set aside.
5. Lemon Filling: In a medium saucepan, whisk together the granulated sugar, cornstarch, and salt.
6. Gradually whisk in the lemon juice, lemon zest, non-dairy milk, and turmeric (if using). Continue to whisk until the mixture is smooth and well combined.
7. Place the saucepan over medium heat and cook the mixture, stirring constantly, until it thickens. This should take about 8-10 minutes. The filling should coat the back of a spoon.
8. Once the filling is thickened, pour it over the baked crust in the baking pan.
9. Return the pan to the oven and bake for an additional 20-25 minutes, or until the filling is set and the edges are lightly golden.
10. Remove the pan from the oven and let it cool completely on a wire rack.
11. Once the lemon bars are completely cooled, dust the top with powdered sugar.
12. Carefully remove the bars from the pan and cut them into squares or rectangles.
13. Serve your vegan lemon bars as a delicious and tangy dessert!

BLUEBERRY MUFFIN

Here's a little useless trivia for you: the blueberry muffin is the official State Muffin of Minnesota (New York's is the apple muffin. I know, could I be any nerdier?). So, Minnesotans, this blueberry muffin recipe is for you. Or anyone else who wants a warm, soft treat. I've added a touch of lemon for some zest. And since blueberries are a superfood, we can pretend it's super healthy. I hope this recipe makes Minnesota proud.

PREPARATION TIME
15 MINUTES

COOKING TIME
20-25 MINUTES

SERVES
12 MUFFINS

INGREDIENTS

- 2 cups all-purpose flour
- 1/2 cup granulated sugar
- 2 tsp baking powder
- 1/2 tsp baking soda
- 1/4 tsp salt
- 1 cup non-dairy milk (e.g., almond milk, soy milk)
- 1/3 cup vegetable oil
- 1 tsp vanilla extract
- 1 cup fresh or frozen blueberries
- 1 tbsp all-purpose flour (for coating blueberries)
- Optional: lemon zest or cinnamon (for extra flavor)

DIRECTIONS

1. Preheat your oven to 375°F (190°C). Line a muffin tin with paper liners or lightly grease the cups.
2. In a bowl, toss the blueberries with 1 tbsp of flour. This will help prevent them from sinking to the bottom of the muffins.
3. In a large mixing bowl, whisk together the all-purpose flour, granulated sugar, baking powder, baking soda, and salt.
4. In a separate bowl, mix together the non-dairy milk, vegetable oil, and vanilla extract.
5. Gradually pour the wet ingredients into the dry ingredients and mix until just combined. Do not overmix; a few lumps are okay.
6. Gently fold in the coated blueberries. If you're adding lemon zest or cinnamon, this is the time to add them.
7. Using a spoon or an ice cream scoop, divide the muffin batter evenly among the muffin cups, filling each about 2/3 full.
8. Bake the muffins in the preheated oven for about 20-25 minutes, or until a toothpick inserted into the center of a muffin comes out clean or with a few crumbs (but not wet batter).
9. Remove the muffin tin from the oven and let the muffins cool in the tin for a few minutes before transferring them to a wire rack to cool completely.
10. Once the muffins are completely cooled, enjoy your delicious vegetarian blueberry muffins!

VEGAN TIRAMISU TRUFFLES

As a busy chef and world traveler, I could always use a good "pick me up." Which is what tiramisu means in Italian. It's a layered, coffee-flavored dessert that I can't get enough of. On the other hand, chocolate truffles were invented in France on Christmas Day 1895, when a French baker named Louis Dufour whipped them up to boost holiday sales (I can imagine how those sales skyrocketed after the first bite!). This recipe combines the best of both desserts, giving you a rich chocolate and pleasing coffee flavor. It really is the ultimate pick me up.

PREPARATION TIME
20 MINUTES

COOKING TIME
10 MINUTES

CHILL TIME
45 MINUTES

SERVES
20 TRUFFLES

INGREDIENTS

Chocolate coating:
- 1 1/2 cups (270 g) of vegan semi-sweet chocolate chips
- 1/2 cup coconut cream
- 2 tbsp espresso shot

Truffle:
- 1 cup plus 2 tbsp almond flour
- 1 drop of almond extract optional
- 4 tbsp vegan cream cheese
- 4 tbsp maple syrup
- 1/8 tsp salt
- 1 tsp lemon juice
- 4 tbsp cocoa powder for rolling

DIRECTIONS

1. Put the coconut cream and espresso to a saucepan and bring to a boil.
2. Turn off the heat and add the chocolate chips in. Let them sit for a few seconds, and then whisk until the chocolate is melted evenly. Set aside. If it is too thin, then refrigerate it for 10 minutes.
3. For the truffle mixture, mix all the ingredients in a bowl. Add more almond flour as needed. If it's still too sticky, add in a tsp of neutral flour such as oat flour, and mix in. Refrigerate this mixture for 15 minutes so that it stiffens up a little bit.
4. Take scoops of the cheese mixture and make it into half-inch balls, then coat these balls in the melted chocolate mixture and set it on parchment. Repeat for all of the mixture. Chill these balls for 15 minutes so that the chocolate sets and hardens a little bit. You can just put them in the freezer for faster setting. Then dip them in the chocolate again. The double-dipping creates a thick fudgy chocolate coating. You don't have to make them look pretty or even, because we are going to eventually roll them up. So however the shape is, just coat them in the thick chocolate mixture, and set them on parchment, and let them chill for another 15-20 minutes, or until they are nicely set.
5. Now take all of these truffles out, add two tbsp of cocoa powder in a shallow bowl.
6. Take each truffle and roll it between your palms so that it is an even sphere. The heat of your palms will help warm the chocolate and even it out. Roll them in the cocoa powder and set aside. Keep these truffles refrigerated until ready to serve.

CARROT CAKE

Given my plant-based diet, carrot cake should be my favorite cake by a wide margin. Unfortunately, I can't eat most carrot cake recipes. But I can really tear into this one. And you can, too, whether you're vegan or not. Carrot cake is believed to have originated in Medieval Europe, where sugar and other sweeteners were luxury items. Carrots (which the Moors introduced to Europe) were used as a substitute. And even though sugar is no longer scarce, shredded carrots are a great addition to a spice cake.

PREPARATION TIME
20 MINUTES

COOKING TIME
30-35 MINUTES

SERVES
8-10 SERVINGS

INGREDIENTS

For the Cake:
- 2 cups all-purpose flour
- 1 1/2 cups granulated sugar
- 2 tsp baking powder
- 1 tsp baking soda
- 1/2 tsp salt
- 1 tsp ground cinnamon
- 1/2 tsp ground nutmeg
- 1/2 cup vegetable oil
- 1 1/2 cups grated carrots
- 1 cup unsweetened applesauce
- 1 tsp vanilla extract

- 1/2 cup chopped walnuts or pecans (optional)
- 1/2 cup raisins (optional)

For the Vegan Cream Cheese Frosting:
- 1/2 cup vegan cream cheese (store-bought or homemade)
- 1/4 cup vegan butter, softened
- 2 cups powdered sugar
- 1 tsp vanilla extract

DIRECTIONS

1. Preheat your oven to 350°F (175°C). Grease and flour two 8-inch round cake pans or line them with parchment paper for easy removal.
2. Cake: In a large mixing bowl, whisk together the all-purpose flour, granulated sugar, baking powder, baking soda, salt, ground cinnamon, and ground nutmeg.
3. In a separate bowl, mix together the vegetable oil, grated carrots, unsweetened applesauce, and vanilla extract.
4. Gradually add the wet ingredients to the dry ingredients and mix until well combined. If using, fold in the chopped walnuts or pecans and raisins.
5. Divide the cake batter evenly between the prepared cake pans.
6. Bake the cakes in the preheated oven for about 30-35 minutes, or until a toothpick inserted into the center of the cakes comes out clean.
7. Remove the cakes from the oven and let them cool in the pans for a few minutes before transferring them to a wire rack to cool completely.
8. Vegan Cream Cheese Frosting: In a mixing bowl, beat the vegan cream cheese and softened vegan butter until creamy and well combined.
9. Gradually add the powdered sugar and continue to beat until the frosting is smooth and fluffy.
10. Stir in the vanilla extract.
11. Once the cakes are completely cooled, spread a layer of the vegan cream cheese frosting on top of one cake layer.
12. Place the second cake layer on top and frost the top and sides of the cake with the remaining cream cheese frosting.
13. Optional: Garnish the cake with additional grated carrots, chopped nuts, or edible flowers.
14. Slice and enjoy your delicious vegan carrot cake!

RICE CRISPY TREATS

Rice Krispie Treats are a Midwestern dessert through and through. They were invented in Battle Creek Michigan - home of Kellogg - by two of the company's employees. Developed in 1939, they were used to promote the fledgling cereal. 84 years later, I'd say the promotion was a success. This classic vegetarian dessert can easily be made vegan by substituting vegan butter for the standard variety. Either way, this tasty treat is sure to please.

VEGETARIAN

PREPARATION TIME
10 MINUTES

COOKING TIME
5 MINUTES

SERVES
12 TREATS

INGREDIENTS

- 4 cups crispy rice cereal
- 4 cups mini marshmallows (check for vegetarian marshmallows if desired)
- 3 tbsp unsalted butter or vegan butter
- 1 tsp vanilla extract
- Pinch of salt (omit if using salted butter)
- Cooking spray or additional butter for greasing the pan

DIRECTIONS

1. Grease a 9x9-inch baking pan with cooking spray or use a little butter to prevent sticking.
2. In a large pot, melt the unsalted butter (or vegan butter) over low heat.
3. Add the mini marshmallows to the melted butter and stir constantly until the marshmallows are completely melted and smooth.
4. Remove the pot from the heat and stir in the vanilla extract and a pinch of salt, if using.
5. Quickly add the crispy rice cereal to the melted marshmallow mixture and gently fold it in until the cereal is fully coated.
6. Transfer the mixture to the prepared baking pan.
7. Use a greased spatula or your hands (lightly greased) to press the mixture evenly into the pan.
8. Allow the treats to cool and set at room temperature for about 30 minutes.
9. Once the treats are completely cooled and set, use a sharp knife to cut them into squares or rectangles.
10. Enjoy your tasty vegetarian rice crispy treats with melted chocolate for an extra yummy treat!

PEACH COBBLER

Those who have been following my blog know that I have done some serious traveling in Georgia. When I'm there, I have to do two things: chow down on (vegan) BBQ and stuff my face with all peach everything. Of course, one of my favorite peach dishes is the classic peach cobbler. They've been baking this sweet treat in the South since the late 18th century, and this dish combines aspects of my favorite recipes. It's a proudly old-fashioned recipe, no bells and whistles here. Just that classic scratch-made goodness.

100% VEGAN

PREPARATION TIME
15 MINUTES

COOKING TIME
45 MINUTES

SERVES
6 SERVINGS

INGREDIENTS

For the Peach Filling:
- 5-6 medium peaches, peeled, pitted, and sliced
- 1/4 cup granulated sugar
- 1 tbsp cornstarch
- 1 tsp lemon juice
- 1/2 tsp vanilla extract
- 1/2 tsp ground cinnamon

For the Cobbler Topping:
- 1 cup all-purpose flour
- 1/4 cup granulated sugar
- 1 1/2 tsp baking powder
- 1/4 tsp salt
- 1/3 cup vegan butter, melted
- 1/3 cup non-dairy milk (e.g., almond milk, soy milk)
- 1 tsp vanilla extract

DIRECTIONS

1. Preheat your oven to 375°F (190°C).
2. Peach Filling: In a mixing bowl, combine the sliced peaches, granulated sugar, cornstarch, lemon juice, vanilla extract, and ground cinnamon. Toss until the peaches are coated in the mixture.
3. Transfer the peach mixture to a greased 9x9-inch baking dish or a similar-sized baking dish.
4. Cobbler Topping: In another bowl, whisk together the all-purpose flour, granulated sugar, baking powder, and salt.
5. Add the melted vegan butter, non-dairy milk, and vanilla extract to the dry ingredients. Mix until just combined; do not overmix.
6. Drop spoonfuls of the cobbler topping over the peach mixture in the baking dish. It's okay if the topping is not perfectly spread out; it will expand as it bakes.
7. Place the baking dish in the preheated oven and bake for about 40-45 minutes, or until the topping is golden brown and the peach filling is bubbling.
8. Remove the cobbler from the oven and let it cool for a few minutes before serving.
9. Serve your vegan peach cobbler warm, either on its own or with a scoop of vegan vanilla ice cream or whipped cream.
10. Enjoy this delicious and comforting dessert!

RATATOUILLE

As I mentioned on my blog, Ratatouille is one of my favorite movies. It also happens to be one of my favorite dishes. It's fresh, complex (but not complicated), and naturally vegan. It began as a humble peasant dish in the farming communities around Nice, France. And you'd better believe I ate my fill of it when I traveled to France. Now, you can too–no passport required.

PREPARATION TIME
20 MINUTES

COOKING TIME
10 MINUTES

SERVES
4 SERVINGS

INGREDIENTS

- 5 tbsp olive oil, divided, plus more for serving
- 3 to 4 medium yellow summer squash (about 1 1/2 pounds), large dice
- 1 large bell pepper, large dice
- 1 large green squash, diced
- 1 cup kalamata olives
- 1 1/2 pounds eggplant (1 large), large dice

- Kosher salt
- Freshly ground black pepper
- 1 medium yellow onion, diced
- 2 cloves garlic, minced
- 2 sprigs of fresh thyme
- 1 bay leaf
- 1 pound tomatoes (4-5 medium),
- 1/4 cup loosely packed fresh basil leaves, thinly sliced, plus more for serving

DIRECTIONS

1. Cut a small "X" into the bottom of 3 of the Roma tomatoes, and prepare both a pot of boiling water and a large bowl of ice water.
2. Blanch the tomatoes for less than one minute, until cuts just begin to split up the sides of the tomatoes. Remove immediately and place in the ice bath, and allow to cool completely. Set aside.
3. Set a large stovetop gas burner to high, and place two bell peppers directly on the grate over the flame. Allow to char completely before flipping, and blackening on all sides.
4. Remove from heat and cover with tin foil for about 5 minutes, until softened. Peel off skins.
5. Place in a high-powered blender or food processor, along with remaining tomatoes, the picked leaves of one rosemary sprig, thyme, garlic, onion, vegetable stock, water, kalamata olives, and 1 tbsp olive oil. Blend on high speed until completely smooth.
6. Preheat oven to 225°F.
7. Using a very sharp knife, cut the remaining tomatoes into 1/8-inch thick slices, and place on a parchment-lined baking sheet.
8. Using a mandolin, slice the squash into 1/8-inch thick slices, and stack on the baking sheet.
9. In a shallow roaster or casserole, pour a thin layer of the roast pepper mixture, and spread evenly. Begin shingling vegetables on top: eggplant, followed by tomato, yellow squash, and green squash – continuing the pattern around the edge of the roaster, letting each slice stick out less than 1/4-inch from underneath the following slice.
10. Once the outside of the roaster has been lined with vegetables, repeat another layer inside, and continue until the roaster is filled with patterned vegetables.
11. Finely chop the remaining rosemary, and sprinkle over top with 1 tbsp olive oil, salt, and pepper.
12. Cut a piece of parchment paper to the size of the roaster, place on top of vegetables.
13. Roast for 90 minutes, removing the parchment paper during the final 20 minutes of cooking.
14. Once vegetables are completely softened but still hold their shape, remove from the oven.
15. Place a ring mold in the center of a large plate, and fill widthwise with vegetables stacked vertically.
16. Place a layer of vegetables staggered horizontally over top, and slowly remove ring mold.
17. Combine 1 tbsp of the red pepper sauce from the bottom of the roaster with the remaining olive oil, and drizzle in a circle around the outside of the vegetable stack. Garnish with torn parsley and serve.

CREME BRULEE

Is there a more satisfying dessert than crème brûlée? It has a deep, rich flavor and the perfect textural contrast between the soft custard and hard, sugary shell. "Crème brûlée" is French for "burnt cream," and the term first appears in a 1691 French cookbook called "Le Cuisinier Royal et Bourgeois," by Francois Massialot, who cooked at Versailles. This truly is a dessert fit for a king. And you'll feel like royalty, too, when you dive in!

PREPARATION TIME
15 MINUTES

COOKING TIME
45 MINUTES (PLUS CHILLING TIME)

SERVES
4 SERVINGS

INGREDIENTS

- 2 cups heavy cream
- 1 vanilla bean or 1 tsp vanilla extract
- 4 large egg yolks
- 1/2 cup granulated sugar
- Extra granulated sugar for caramelizing

DIRECTIONS

1. Preheat your oven to 325°F (165°C). Place four ramekins in a baking dish.
2. Cream Mixture: In a saucepan, heat the heavy cream over medium heat until it starts to steam. If using a vanilla bean, split it lengthwise and scrape out the seeds. Add the vanilla bean pod and seeds (or vanilla extract) to the cream. Let the mixture steep for about 10 minutes, then remove the vanilla bean pod.
3. Egg Yolk Mixture: In a mixing bowl, whisk together the egg yolks and granulated sugar until the mixture becomes pale and slightly thickened.
4. Combining Mixtures: Slowly pour the warm cream mixture into the egg yolk mixture while constantly whisking. This is to temper the egg yolks and prevent them from curdling.
5. Straining: Strain the mixture through a fine-mesh sieve into a pitcher or a bowl with a spout. This will help remove any potential bits of cooked egg or vanilla bean.
6. Filling Ramekins: Divide the strained mixture evenly among the four ramekins.
7. Baking: Place the baking dish with the ramekins in the preheated oven. Carefully pour hot water into the baking dish to create a water bath that comes about halfway up the sides of the ramekins.
8. Bake the crème brûlées for about 35-40 minutes, or until they are set around the edges but still slightly jiggly in the center.
9. Chilling: Carefully remove the ramekins from the water bath and let them cool to room temperature. Then, cover them with plastic wrap and refrigerate for at least 2 hours or until they are thoroughly chilled.
10. Caramelizing the Top: Just before serving, sprinkle a thin layer of granulated sugar evenly over the top of each crème brûlée. Use a kitchen torch to carefully caramelize the sugar until it's golden brown and crisp.
11. Serving: Let the caramelized sugar cool and harden for a minute before serving your vegetarian crème brûlée.
12. Enjoy the creamy and decadent delight of your homemade vegetarian crème brûlée!

DOLMADES

Stuffed grape leaves, or dolmades, have been a staple in the Mediterranean region for centuries. This particular recipe draws on the many dolmades I ate while in Greece. Few dishes capture the fresh, rustic flavors of the Mediterranean better than dolmades. And while many recipes call for ground meat, this recipe should please every foodie at your table.

PREPARATION TIME
30 MINUTES

COOKING TIME
45 MINUTES

SERVES
20-24 DOLMADES

INGREDIENTS

- 1 cup uncooked rice (preferably short-grain rice)
- 1/4 cup olive oil
- 1 large onion, finely chopped
- 1/4 cup pine nuts
- 1/4 cup raisins
- 2 tbsp chopped fresh dill
- 2 tbsp chopped fresh mint

- 2 tbsp chopped fresh parsley
- Juice of 1 lemon
- Salt and pepper, to taste
- About 20-24 grape leaves (canned or fresh)
- Water, for boiling
- Lemon slices and fresh herbs for garnish (optional)

DIRECTIONS

1. Rice Filling: In a large skillet, heat the olive oil over medium heat. Add the chopped onion and sauté until translucent.
2. Add the pine nuts to the skillet and toast them until they are lightly golden.
3. Stir in the uncooked rice and sauté for a couple of minutes, coating the rice with the oil and onions.
4. Add the raisins, chopped dill, chopped mint, and chopped parsley to the skillet. Mix well to combine.
5. Pour in the lemon juice and season with salt and pepper. Mix everything together and remove from the heat. Allow the rice filling to cool slightly.
6. Preparing Grape Leaves: If using fresh grape leaves, blanch them in boiling water for a few seconds to soften them. If using canned grape leaves, rinse and drain them to remove excess brine.
7. Rolling Dolmades: Lay a grape leaf flat, vein side up. Place a small spoonful of the rice filling near the stem end of the leaf.
8. Fold the sides of the leaf over the filling and then roll from the stem end to the tip, creating a compact and tidy roll.
9. Repeat this process with the remaining grape leaves and rice filling.
10. Cooking Dolmades: Line the bottom of a large pot with any torn or leftover grape leaves to prevent the dolmades from sticking. Arrange the rolled dolmades in the pot, seam side down, in a single layer.
11. Pour enough water over the dolmades to cover them. Place a heavy plate on top to keep the dolmades from floating.
12. Cover the pot and bring the water to a boil. Reduce the heat to low and let the dolmades simmer gently for about 30-35 minutes or until the rice is cooked.
13. Serving: Carefully remove the dolmades from the pot and arrange them on a serving platter. Garnish with lemon slices and fresh herbs if desired.
14. Serve your delicious vegan dolmades warm or at room temperature as an appetizer or side dish.

STUFFED MUSHROOMS

Stuffed mushrooms have become a popular appetizer/hors d'oeuvre in recent years, but this is actually a rather old dish that hails from Italy. In fact, serving stuffed mushrooms on Thanksgiving is a popular tradition for many Italian-American families (one I will definitely be adopting). But this simple recipe, which brings in rich flavors from olive oil and butter, is good any time of the year.

100% VEGAN

PREPARATION TIME
15 MINUTES

COOKING TIME
10 MINUTES

SERVES
4 SERVINGS

INGREDIENTS

- 12 button mushrooms
- 1 red onion
- 1 tbsp of olive oil
- 12 almonds
- 1 large tbsp of butter
- A few sprigs of parsley
- 1 pinch of salt
- 1 pinch of ground black pepper

DIRECTIONS

1. Quickly wash the mushrooms with a damp sponge or a small, damp, soft brush to avoid breaking them.
2. Remove the ends of the mushrooms.
3. Preheat the oven to 350°F.
4. Place the mushrooms on a sheet of parchment or silicone paper.
5. Sprinkle them with salt and bake for 15 minutes.
6. Peel the onion and chop it. Fry it in a little olive oil.
7. Finely chop the stems of the mushrooms.
8. Add the sliced mushroom stems. Continue cooking over low heat until the onion is tender.
9. Once out of the oven, drain the water from the mushroom caps.
10. Put the onion, mushroom stems, butter, almonds, parsley, salt, and pepper in a blender.
11. Mix the whole mixture of ingredients together.
12. Fill the mushrooms with the prepared stuffing.
13. Bake again for 15 minutes. Remove from the oven and let cool for 5 minutes.
14. Serve hot or lukewarm, and enjoy your appetizer!

BANGERS AND MASH

I'm sure most of us have heard the term "Bangers and Mash"; perhaps even ordered the dish at a British-style pub. "Bangers" are, of course, sausages, and "mash" refers to mashed potatoes. The origin of the term "bangers" is an interesting one: during World War I, sausages were made with such a high water content (due to the rationing of meat) that they often popped when cooked. The resulting bang is where the name comes from. The days of war rationing are long gone, but the name stuck. And because this recipe is meatless, the right ingredients should be easy to come by, rations or not.

VEGETARIAN
VEGETARIAN

PREPARATION TIME
15 MINUTES

COOKING TIME
30 MINUTES

SERVES
4 SERVINGS

INGREDIENTS

For the Vegetarian Sausages ("Bangers"):
- 4 vegetarian sausages (such as plant-based or tofu sausages)
- 2 tbsp olive oil

For the Mashed Potatoes ("Mash"):
- 4 large potatoes, peeled and cut into chunks
- 1/4 cup unsweetened non-dairy milk (e.g., almond milk, oat milk)
- 2 tbsp vegan butter or olive oil
- Salt and pepper, to taste

For the Onion Gravy:
- 1 large onion, thinly sliced
- 2 tbsp olive oil
- 2 tbsp all-purpose flour
- 2 cups vegetable broth
- 1 tbsp soy sauce
- Salt and pepper, to taste

DIRECTIONS

1. Vegetarian Sausages ("Bangers"): In a skillet, heat the olive oil over medium heat. Add the vegetarian sausages and cook according to the package instructions until they are browned and heated through. Set aside.
2. Mashed Potatoes ("Mash"): In a large pot, bring water to a boil. Add the potato chunks and cook until they are fork-tender, about 15-20 minutes.
3. Drain the cooked potatoes and return them to the pot. Add the non-dairy milk and vegan butter (or olive oil). Mash the potatoes using a potato masher or a fork until smooth and creamy. Season with salt and pepper to taste. Keep warm.
4. Onion Gravy: In a separate skillet, heat the olive oil over medium heat. Add the sliced onions and sauté until they are soft and caramelized, about 10-15 minutes.
5. Sprinkle the flour over the onions and stir to coat them evenly.
6. Gradually add the vegetable broth and soy sauce to the skillet, stirring constantly to avoid lumps. Cook the gravy until it thickens and becomes smooth about 5 minutes. Season with salt and pepper to taste.
7. Assembly: Serve a portion of the mashed potatoes on each plate. Top with a vegetarian sausage ("banger") and generously spoon the onion gravy over the sausages and potatoes.
8. Enjoy your comforting and hearty vegetarian bangers and mash!

STICKY TOFFEE PUDDING

Despite its name, Sticky Toffee Pudding is actually a sponge cake covered in a rich toffee sauce and sometimes topped with ice cream. This sweet, moist dessert is classic pub food. In fact, it is said to have originated in a pub in Northwest England (exactly which pub is a matter of dispute). Maybe that's why this dish pairs so wonderfully with a stout or porter! Cheers.

PREPARATION TIME
20 MINUTES

COOKING TIME
30 MINUTES

SERVES
6 SERVINGS

INGREDIENTS

For the Pudding:
- 1 cup dates, pitted and chopped
- 1 cup boiling water
- 1 tsp baking soda
- 1/4 cup vegan butter or coconut oil, melted
- 3/4 cup brown sugar
- 1 tsp vanilla extract
- 1 1/2 cups all-purpose flour
- 1 tsp baking powder
- Pinch of salt

For the Toffee Sauce:
- 1/2 cup brown sugar
- 1/4 cup vegan butter
- 1/2 cup coconut cream (the thick part from a can of full-fat coconut milk)
- Pinch of salt

DIRECTIONS

1. Preheat your oven to 350°F (175°C). Grease a baking dish or individual ramekins.
2. Pudding: In a bowl, place the chopped dates and pour the boiling water over them. Stir in the baking soda and let the mixture sit for about 10 minutes to soften the dates.
3. In a separate bowl, whisk together the melted vegan butter (or coconut oil), brown sugar, and vanilla extract.
4. In another bowl, combine the all-purpose flour, baking powder, and a pinch of salt.
5. Gradually add the wet ingredients to the dry ingredients and mix until just combined.
6. Stir in the date mixture, making sure it's evenly distributed in the batter.
7. Pour the batter into the prepared baking dish or ramekins.
8. Bake in the preheated oven for about 25-30 minutes or until a toothpick inserted into the center of the pudding comes out clean.
9. Toffee Sauce: While the pudding is baking, prepare the toffee sauce. In a saucepan, melt the vegan butter over medium heat. Add the brown sugar and stir until it's dissolved and bubbling.
10. Stir in the coconut cream and a pinch of salt. Simmer the mixture for a few minutes until it thickens slightly.
11. Serving: Once the pudding is baked, remove it from the oven and let it cool slightly.
12. Serve the warm pudding drizzled with the toffee sauce.
13. Optionally, top with a dollop of vegan whipped cream or a scoop of vegan vanilla ice cream.
14. Enjoy your indulgent vegan sticky toffee pudding!

SPRING ROLLS

The spring roll is a dish that goes back hundreds of years. They were first eaten in mainland China to commemorate the start of spring (hence the name). Being a seasonal dish, they were often filled with fresh spring vegetables. A symbol of wealth, spring rolls were traditionally given as gifts. I want to resurrect the custom of giving spring rolls as gifts–I mean, who wouldn't like a plate of them right now? Especially these vegetarian spring rolls, filled with fresh and bioavailable ingredients like carrots, bean sprouts, and white cabbage. Let the gifting begin!

PREPARATION TIME
20 MINUTES

COOKING TIME
15 MINUTES

SERVES
10 SPRING ROLLS

INGREDIENTS

- 50 g glass noodles
- 1 carrot (roughly grated)
- 100g white cabbage (finely grated)
- 100g bean sprout
- 2 cloves garlic (finely chopped)
- 15 ml sesame oil
- Soy sauce (to taste)
- 10 sheets spring roll pastry
- Oil for frying

DIRECTIONS

1. First is cooking the noodles according to the directions on the package.
2. Mix the carrots, cabbage, bean sprouts, garlic, and oil together.
3. Drain the noodles, cut them into 4 cm long pieces, and add them to the mixture.
4. Season with salt, ground black pepper, soy sauce, and a pinch of sugar, and gently beat the egg.
5. Separate one spring roll sheet from the pile and place it on the work surface. Spread 30 ml of filling in the middle.
6. Fold over the sides and roll up.
7. Fry spring rolls in hot oil for 5 minutes until golden brown.
8. Dry on kitchen paper.
9. Serve the spring rolls with spicy vinegar sauce.

SWEET AND SOUR STICKY TOFU

Chinese cooking is all about balancing flavor contrasts. One of the most famous contrasts in Chinese cuisine is that of sweet and sour. Dishes like sweet and sour chicken/pork have become a mainstay at Chinese restaurants here in the States. These dishes were likely introduced by the Cantonese immigrants who came here to build the railroads in the late 19th century, many of whom turned to cooking to circumvent oppressive laws (restaurant owners could travel back and forth to China on a merchant visa; most laborers could not). This dish honors the contributions of Chinese migrants in America. And even though I've substituted tofu for the traditional chicken or pork, the flavor profile should take you back to some of those first meals at your local Chinese restaurant.

PREPARATION TIME
15 MINUTES

COOKING TIME
40 MINUTES

SERVES
2 SERVINGS

INGREDIENTS

- 20g cashew nuts
- 2 brown onions
- 1-2 red chillies
- 1 1/4 tbsp apple cider vinegar
- 1 tbsp maple syrup
- 2 tbsp oil (divided)

- 1 tbsp tamari
- 1 yellow pepper
- 2 1/2 tbsp tomato puree
- 400g firm tofu
- 50g kale
- 5 tsp cornflour
- 80g rice

DIRECTIONS

1. Preheat the oven to 180°C (350°F) or gas mark 4. Also, boil a kettle of water. Rinse the rice and place it into a saucepan with 450ml of boiling water and a pinch of sea salt. Simmer for 25 minutes until cooked, then drain.
2. Chop the yellow pepper and onion into bite-sized pieces. Roughly chop the kale. Finely chop the chili (remove the seeds for less heat). Drain and rinse the tofu, then pat it dry with paper towels. Cut the tofu into 2cm cubes.
3. Make a sweet and sour sauce by mixing the tamari, tomato puree, maple syrup, apple cider vinegar, and half of the chopped chili together with 2 tbsp of cold water in a small bowl.
4. Place the cornflour into a bowl with a pinch of sea salt. Toss the tofu cubes in the cornflour to coat them evenly.
5. Place the kale on a baking tray with a pinch of sea salt and combine with 1 tsp of oil. Spread it out into an even layer. Place it in the oven for 10-15 minutes until it turns crispy.
6. Heat a large wok or pan with 2 tsp of oil over medium-high heat. Add the coated tofu and cook for 10-15 minutes, turning occasionally until the tofu turns golden brown.
7. Add the chopped onion and pepper to the wok and cook for 3-5 minutes until they start to soften.
8. Pour in the sweet and sour sauce and reduce the heat. Cook for an additional 2 minutes until the sauce thickens.
9. Spoon the cooked rice into two warm bowls. Place the sweet and sour tofu on the side and add the crispy kale.
10. Sprinkle the dish with cashew nuts and the remaining chopped chili if desired.
11. Serve and enjoy your flavorful sweet and sour tofu with crispy kale over rice!

MASALA

I'm sure you've seen "chicken tikka masala" (a dish that actually originated in the Indian restaurants of Great Britain) on Indian menus here in the U.S. "Masala" is simply the Hindi word for "spice," and it can be used to describe dry, wet, ground, or whole spices. For my vegan masala lentils, we'll be using a variety of classic Indian spices, including cumin, coriander, cinnamon, and cardamom (this recipe is brought to you by the letter C!). And lentils being a superfood, this is a very healthy, nutritious dish that you shouldn't feel guilty about eating by the bowlful.

PREPARATION TIME
15 MINUTES

COOKING TIME
25 MINUTES

SERVES
4 SERVINGS

INGREDIENTS

- 2 cups mixed vegetables (such as potatoes, carrots, peas, bell peppers), chopped
- 1 cup canned chickpeas, drained and rinsed
- 1 onion, finely chopped
- 2 tomatoes, finely chopped
- 2 cloves garlic, minced
- 1-inch piece of ginger, grated
- 2 tbsp vegetable oil
- 1 tsp cumin seeds
- 1 tsp ground coriander

- 1/2 tsp ground cumin
- 1/2 tsp turmeric
- 1/2 tsp paprika
- 1/4 tsp ground cinnamon
- 1/4 tsp ground cardamom
- 1/4 tsp cayenne pepper (adjust to taste)
- 1/2 cup plain yogurt (vegan yogurt for a vegan version)
- 1/4 cup chopped cilantro (coriander leaves)
- Salt, to taste

DIRECTIONS

1. In a large skillet or pan, heat the vegetable oil over medium heat.
2. Add the cumin seeds and let them sizzle for a few seconds until fragrant.
3. Add the chopped onion and sauté until it becomes soft and translucent.
4. Stir in the minced garlic and grated ginger. Sauté for another minute until fragrant.
5. Add the chopped tomatoes to the skillet. Cook and stir until the tomatoes break down and become soft.
6. Lower the heat and add the ground coriander, ground cumin, turmeric, paprika, ground cinnamon, ground cardamom, and cayenne pepper. Mix well to combine the spices with the tomato mixture.
7. Stir in the mixed vegetables and canned chickpeas. Cook for a few minutes until the vegetables start to soften.
8. Add a splash of water if the mixture becomes too dry.
9. Pour in the plain yogurt and gently mix it into the vegetables. Cook for a few more minutes, allowing the flavors to meld.
10. Season the masala with salt to taste.
11. Just before serving, sprinkle chopped cilantro over the masala.
12. Serve your flavorful vegetarian masala over rice or with naan, roti, or any preferred bread.
13. Enjoy your delicious and aromatic vegetarian masala!

TANDOORI TOFU

As I got more into cooking, I came to appreciate traditional recipes and cooking methods. The people of the Indian subcontinent have been cooking with tandoors (traditionally large, round clay ovens) for thousands of years. These ovens reach an extremely high temperature (up to 900 degrees Fahrenheit) for quick cooking and a wonderful char. I don't expect you to have a tandoor in your kitchen, but this recipe allows you to replicate those smoky, charred South Asian flavors at home. You'll never look at tofu the same way again.

PREPARATION TIME
20 MINUTES

COOKING TIME
25 MINUTES

SERVES
4 SERVINGS

INGREDIENTS

For the Tofu Marinade:
- 1 block (14 oz) extra-firm tofu, pressed and cubed
- 1/2 cup dairy-free yogurt (coconut or almond yogurt works well)
- 2 tbsp tandoori masala spice mix
- 1 tbsp lemon juice
- 1 tbsp olive oil
- 1 tsp ground cumin
- 1 tsp paprika
- 1/2 tsp turmeric
- 1/2 tsp ground coriander
- 1/4 tsp cayenne pepper (adjust to taste)
- Salt to taste

For Cooking:
- Skewers (wooden skewers, soaked in water for 30 minutes if using)
- Cooking spray or oil, for grilling

For Serving (optional):
- Chopped fresh cilantro
- Lemon wedges
- Sliced red onions

DIRECTIONS

1. Press the tofu to remove excess moisture. Place the tofu block on a plate lined with paper towels. Place more paper towels on top, and then place a heavy object, like a cast iron skillet, on top of the tofu. Let it press for about 15-20 minutes.
2. Cut the pressed tofu into bite-sized cubes.
3. In a mixing bowl, combine the dairy-free yogurt, tandoori masala spice mix, lemon juice, olive oil, ground cumin, paprika, turmeric, ground coriander, cayenne pepper, and salt. Mix well to form a smooth marinade.
4. Add the tofu cubes to the marinade and gently toss to coat each piece. Make sure all the tofu pieces are well-covered with the marinade.
5. Cover the bowl with plastic wrap or a lid and let the tofu marinate in the refrigerator for at least 2 hours, or ideally overnight. The longer it marinates, the more flavor it will absorb.
6. Preheat your grill to medium-high heat. If you're using wooden skewers, make sure to soak them in water for about 30 minutes to prevent them from burning on the grill.
7. Thread the marinated tofu cubes onto the skewers, leaving a little space between each piece.
8. Lightly grease the grill grates with cooking spray or oil to prevent sticking. Place the tofu skewers on the grill and cook for about 3-4 minutes per side, or until grill marks appear and the tofu is heated through.
9. Once the tofu is cooked, remove the skewers from the grill. Serve the tandoori tofu skewers with chopped cilantro, lemon wedges, and sliced red onions on the side.

LASAGNA

When I went to Rome, I chowed down on lasagna in a way that even Garfield would be jealous of (showing my millennial stripes here). Lasagna is a hearty dish, well suited for feeding a ton of people. And with this vegan lasagna recipe, you will most certainly be the hit of the dinner party. That's because this dish originated in Naples during the Middle Ages and was meant to be served during holidays and festivals. But it's totally OK to whip some up on a random weekday. Just get ready for some serious leftovers.

PREPARATION TIME
30 MINUTES

COOKING TIME
45 MINUTES

SERVES
6-8 SERVINGS

INGREDIENTS

- 12 lasagna noodles
- 2 cups marinara sauce
- 1 tbsp olive oil
- 1 medium onion, chopped
- 2 cloves garlic, minced
- 1 red bell pepper, chopped
- 1 zucchini, chopped
- 1 cup sliced mushrooms

- 1 cup baby spinach
- 1 can (14 oz) crushed tomatoes
- 1 tsp dried oregano
- 1 tsp dried basil
- 1/2 tsp dried thyme
- Salt and pepper to taste
- 2 cups vegan ricotta cheese
- 1 cup shredded vegan mozzarella cheese

DIRECTIONS

1. Preheat the oven to 375°F (190°C).
2. Cook the lasagna noodles according to the package instructions. Once cooked, drain and set aside.
3. In a large skillet, heat the olive oil over medium heat. Add the chopped onion and sauté for about 2-3 minutes, until translucent.
4. Add the minced garlic, red bell pepper, zucchini, and sliced mushrooms to the skillet. Cook for another 5-7 minutes until the vegetables are tender.
5. Pour in the crushed tomatoes and marinara sauce. Add the dried oregano, dried basil, dried thyme, salt, and pepper. Stir to combine, and let the sauce simmer for about 10 minutes.
6. Stir in the baby spinach and cook until it's wilted. Adjust the seasoning as needed.
7. In a bowl, mix together the vegan ricotta cheese with a pinch of salt and pepper.
8. Assemble the lasagna: Spread a thin layer of the sauce mixture on the bottom of a baking dish. Place a layer of lasagna noodles over the sauce. Spread a portion of the vegan ricotta mixture over the noodles. Add another layer of sauce, followed by noodles, and continue layering until all ingredients are used up, finishing with a layer of sauce on top.
9. Sprinkle the shredded vegan mozzarella cheese evenly over the top layer of sauce.
10. Cover the baking dish with aluminum foil and bake in the preheated oven for about 25 minutes.
11. Remove the foil and bake for an additional 10-15 minutes, or until the cheese is melted and bubbly and the edges of the lasagna are golden brown.
12. Once cooked, remove the lasagna from the oven and let it rest for a few minutes before slicing and serving.
13. Serve your delicious vegan lasagna with a side salad, and enjoy!

TIRAMISU

I already included a recipe for delicious tiramisu truffles, but this recipe is a little more classic. This one reminds me of the warm, breezy days I spent sipping espresso and eating tiramisu at outdoor cafes in Italy. And my hope is that when you bite into this tiramisu, you'll be instantly transported to an Italian cafe yourself. It's the next best thing to a plane ticket and a whole lot cheaper.

PREPARATION TIME
30 MINUTES

COOKING TIME
25-30 MINUTES

CHILL TIME
4+ HOURS

SERVES
12 SERVINGS

INGREDIENTS

- 3 cups all-purpose flour
- 1 cup oat milk
- 1 tbsp apple cider vinegar
- 16 oz vegan cream cheese
- 1/2 cup sugar
- 2 tbsp coconut oil
- 1 cup oat milk
- 2 shots espresso
- 2 tbsp coffee liquor
- 2 tsp vanilla extract
- 1 tbsp baking powder
- 2 tbsp cornstarch
- 1 pinch of salt

DIRECTIONS

1. Preheat your oven to 350°F and grease a 10×15 inch sheet pan.
2. Add flour, cornstarch, baking powder, salt, and sugar to a large bowl. Make sure to mix well so that the ingredients combine. Pour canola oil, soy milk, apple cider vinegar, and vanilla extract over the dry ingredients in the bowl and lightly mix.
3. Pour the cake batter into the prepared pan and bake for 25 to 30 minutes or until a toothpick comes out clean.
4. Let the cake cool on a cooling rack.
5. Get a blender and add vegan cream cheese, sugar, coconut oil, a pinch of salt, vanilla, and oat milk. Mix or blend until smooth, then place in the freezer for 10 to 15 minutes. This will help the cream firm up.
6. Make espresso sauce: Add espresso, liquor, and sugar in a medium bowl and then set aside.
7. Get out an 8×8 inch cake pan or a dish with tall edges or walls. Dip each cake strip into the espresso mixture and place it on the bottom of the pan. Continue until there is an even layer of cake. Use a spatula to scoop half of your vegan cream on top of the cake and spread until it reaches the pan edges. Add another layer of espresso-dipped cake pieces, then the rest of the cream, and refrigerate.
8. Leave the cake in the refrigerator for several hours or overnight to let the cream firm up, and the flavors mingle. When you're ready to serve, use a sifter to dust the top of the cake with cocoa powder.

CORNMEAL FRITTERS

As you may know, I have Jamaican ancestry on my father's side. This cookbook would not be complete without paying homage to those roots (it doesn't hurt that I'm absolutely in love with Jamaican cuisine). One classic Jamaican recipe I had to include was cornmeal fritters. It's a quick, simple, fried dish that makes a great snack or side. And I was lucky enough to eat them all over Jamaica. Now, whenever I start to feel nostalgic for my time on the island, I whip up a few of these, and all is well.

PREPARATION TIME
15 MINUTES

COOKING TIME
20 MINUTES

SERVES
4-6 SERVINGS

INGREDIENTS

- 1 cup cornmeal
- 1/2 cup all-purpose flour
- 1 tsp baking powder
- 1/2 tsp baking soda
- 1 tsp salt
- 1/2 tsp black pepper
- 1 tsp ground cumin
- 1/2 tsp smoked paprika
- 1 cup fresh or frozen corn kernels
- 1/2 cup finely chopped bell peppers (assorted colors)
- 1/4 cup finely chopped green onions
- 1 cup dairy-free milk (such as almond or soy milk)
- 2 tbsp apple cider vinegar
- 2 tbsp chopped fresh cilantro (optional)
- Oil for frying

DIRECTIONS

1. In a mixing bowl, combine the cornmeal, all-purpose flour, baking powder, baking soda, salt, black pepper, ground cumin, and smoked paprika.
2. Add the corn kernels, chopped bell peppers, and chopped green onions to the dry ingredients. Mix well to evenly distribute the vegetables in the dry mixture.
3. In a separate bowl, whisk together the dairy-free milk and apple cider vinegar. Let it sit for a few minutes to curdle slightly.
4. Pour the wet mixture into the dry mixture. Stir gently until just combined. Do not overmix; a few lumps are okay. If desired, fold in the chopped cilantro.
5. In a large skillet, heat about 1/2 inch of oil over medium heat. The oil should be hot enough that a small drop of batter sizzles when dropped into it.
6. Using a spoon or a small ice cream scoop, carefully drop spoonfuls of the batter into the hot oil. Flatten the fritters slightly with the back of the spoon.
7. Fry the fritters for about 2-3 minutes on each side, or until they are golden brown and crispy. You may need to adjust the heat slightly to ensure they cook evenly without burning.
8. Use a slotted spoon to remove the fritters from the oil and place them on a plate lined with paper towels to drain any excess oil.
9. Serve the vegan cornmeal fritters warm as a delicious appetizer or snack. They can be enjoyed on their own or with your favorite dipping sauce.

BLACK-EYED PEA CURRY

It is believed that curry was brought to Jamaica (and other Caribbean islands) by indentured workers from India who worked the sugar plantations. Black-eyed peas, on the other hand, are native to North Africa and were brought to the Caribbean through colonial trade routes. This dish is, therefore, a testament to the many cultures that have contributed to Jamaican cuisine. And since my heritage reflects a mishmash of cultures, including Jamaican culture, dishes like this will always have a special place in my heart. And I have a sneaking suspicion it will work its way into your heart, too.

PREPARATION TIME
15 MINUTES

COOKING TIME
30 MINUTES

SERVES
4 SERVINGS

INGREDIENTS

- 2 cups cooked black-eyed peas (canned or cooked from dried)
- 1 tbsp oil (such as vegetable or coconut oil)
- 1 onion, finely chopped
- 2 cloves garlic, minced
- 1 tsp grated ginger
- 1 tsp ground cumin
- 1 tsp ground coriander

- 1/2 tsp turmeric powder
- 1/2 tsp red chili powder (adjust to taste)
- 1 tsp garam masala
- 1 tsp paprika
- 1 can (14 oz) diced tomatoes
- 1 cup coconut milk
- 1 cup vegetable broth
- Salt to taste
- Chopped fresh cilantro for garnish

DIRECTIONS

1. If you're using dried black-eyed peas, soak them overnight and cook them until tender. If using canned black-eyed peas, make sure to rinse and drain them.
2. In a large skillet or pot, heat the oil over medium heat.
3. Add the finely chopped onion and sauté until it becomes translucent.
4. Add the minced garlic and grated ginger. Sauté for about 1-2 minutes until fragrant.
5. Stir in the ground cumin, ground coriander, turmeric powder, red chili powder, garam masala, and paprika. Cook the spices for about 1 minute, stirring constantly to toast them.
6. Add the diced tomatoes (with their juices) to the skillet. Cook for about 5-7 minutes, allowing the tomatoes to break down and the mixture to thicken.
7. Pour in the coconut milk and vegetable broth. Mix well to combine.
8. Add the cooked black-eyed peas to the skillet. Stir everything together and bring the mixture to a gentle simmer.
9. Allow the curry to simmer for about 15-20 minutes, stirring occasionally, until the flavors meld together and the curry thickens.
10. Season the curry with salt to taste. Adjust the seasoning as needed.
11. Once the curry is ready, remove it from the heat.
12. Serve the vegetarian black-eyed pea curry over cooked rice, quinoa, or with Indian bread such as naan or roti.
13. Garnish with chopped fresh cilantro before serving.

MISO SOUP

Miso is a Japanese soup that brings big umami flavors. It is also the first course in many great Japanese meals, setting the tone for the deliciousness to come. Given my Japanese heritage, eating miso soup (repeatedly) in Japan was an important part of my life's journey. And I ate miso soup all over that country: from rice miso in the north to barley miso in the south. And while I enjoyed all the regional varieties, I can say this with certainty: scratch-made miso soup always beats the pre-packaged stuff. And with this easy recipe, you'll be able to enjoy it fresh without a ton of hassle.

100% VEGAN

PREPARATION TIME
10 MINUTES

COOKING TIME
15 MINUTES

SERVES
4 SERVINGS

INGREDIENTS

- 4 cups vegetable broth
- 1 cup water
- 3-4 shiitake mushrooms sliced
- 1 small carrot peeled and sliced
- 1 small onion diced
- 2 cloves garlic minced
- 2 tbsp white miso paste
- 1/4 cup green onions thinly sliced
- 1/4 cup tofu cubed (optional)

DIRECTIONS

1. In a soup pot, bring the vegetable broth and water to a simmer over medium heat.
2. Add the shiitake mushrooms, carrot, onion, and garlic to the pot. Cook for 10-15 minutes or until the vegetables are tender.
3. Remove the soup from the heat and add the white miso paste. Stir until the miso is fully dissolved.
4. Add the green onions and tofu (if using) to the soup. Stir to combine.
5. Ladle the soup into bowls and serve immediately.

DAIFUKU

While many Japanese meals start with miso soup, many of mine end with Daifuku: a glutinous rice cake (mochi) stuffed with red bean paste. And if you've only ever had frozen, pre-made daifuku, you're missing out. Luckily, this popular confection is deceptively simple to make. Word of warning, though: it's also deceptively difficult to resist.

PREPARATION TIME
1 HOUR (INCLUDING SOAKING TIME)

COOKING TIME
10 MINUTES

SERVES
8 DAIFUKU

INGREDIENTS

For the Sweet Red Bean Filling:
- 1 cup sweetened red bean paste (anko)
- 1 tbsp water (if needed to adjust consistency)

For the Mochi Dough:
- 1 cup glutinous rice flour (mochiko)
- 1/4 cup granulated sugar
- 3/4 cup water
- Potato starch or cornstarch, for dusting

DIRECTIONS

1. If the red bean paste is too thick, you can gently heat it with a tbsp of water in a saucepan over low heat, stirring until it reaches a smooth consistency. Allow it to cool.
2. In a microwave-safe bowl, whisk together the glutinous rice flour and sugar. Gradually add the water while stirring to form a smooth paste. It will be quite thick.
3. Cover the bowl with plastic wrap or a microwave-safe lid. Microwave the dough on high for 1 minute. Remove from the microwave and stir the dough with a wet spatula. It will be sticky.
4. Re-cover the bowl and microwave the dough for another 30 seconds. Remove from the microwave and stir again.
5. Liberally dust a clean surface with potato starch or cornstarch. Turn the mochi dough out onto the starch.
6. Coat your hands with starch and knead the warm mochi dough gently until it becomes smooth and pliable. Divide the dough into 8 equal portions.
7. Take one portion of mochi dough and flatten it into a small circle in the palm of your hand. Place a small spoonful of sweet red bean paste in the center. Gently wrap the mochi around the filling, pinching to seal. Roll it into a smooth ball.
8. Repeat the process with the remaining dough and filling.
9. Place the assembled daifuku on a plate lined with parchment paper or dusted with starch. Refrigerate for at least 1 hour to allow the mochi to set.
10. Once chilled, the vegetarian daifuku are ready to be enjoyed. Dust them lightly with potato starch or cornstarch to prevent sticking.
11. You can also roll the daifuku in additional coatings such as matcha powder, cocoa powder, or toasted soybean flour (kinako) for added flavor and texture.

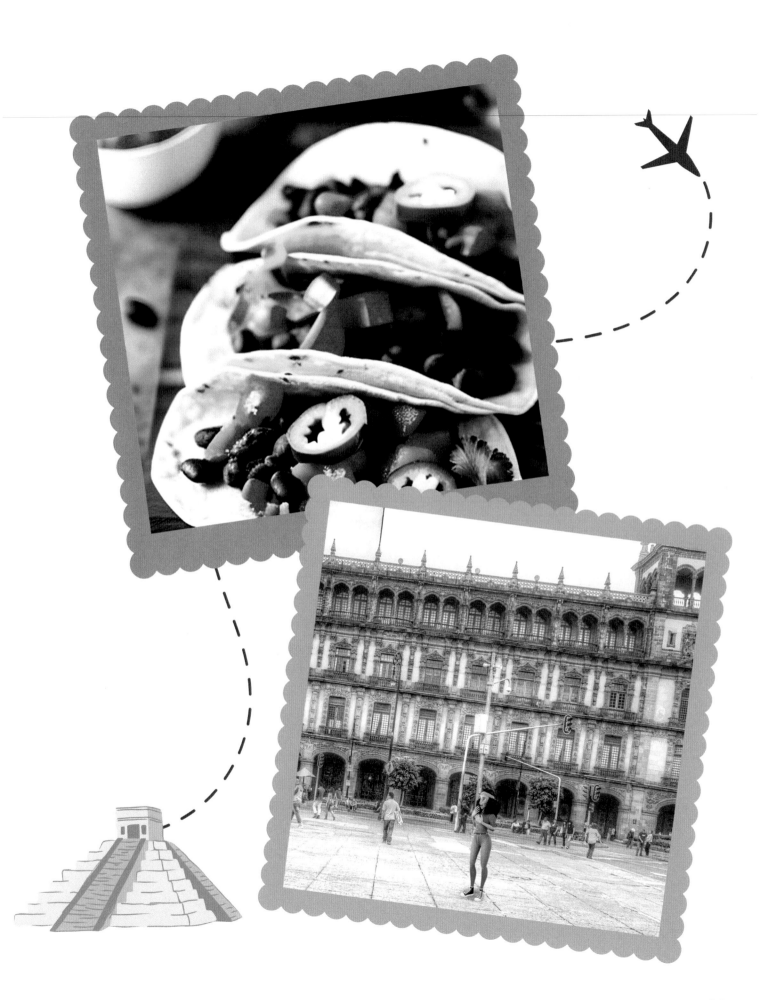

TACOS

Tacos have been a staple in Mexico for hundreds of years. These days, they are pretty much a staple here in the U.S. as well (how many dishes have their own day, a la "Taco Tuesday"). One of the things I love most about tacos is that they're extremely customizable: start with a well-made (ideally fresh) tortilla, add some bright, flavorful salsa, and the filling is pretty much up to you. I honestly can't count how many varieties of vegan tacos I came across (and quickly devoured) while in Mexico. This recipe is one of my favorites–a colorful, flavorful combination of black beans, avocado, dry spices, and a ton of fresh condiments. Taco Tuesday will never be the same.

PREPARATION TIME
10 MINUTES

COOKING TIME
15 MINUTES

SERVES
4 SERVINGS

INGREDIENTS

- 1 tbsp olive oil
- 1 onion diced
- 2 cloves garlic minced
- 1 red bell pepper diced
- 1 jalapeño pepper diced
- 1 can black beans drained and rinsed
- 1 tsp chili powder
- 1 tsp ground cumin
- Salt and pepper to taste
- 8-12 small corn tortillas

Toppings:
- 1 avocado sliced
- 1/4 cup chopped fresh cilantro
- 1/4 cup diced tomatoes
- 1/4 cup diced red onion

- Lime wedges for serving

DIRECTIONS

1. In a skillet, heat olive oil over medium-high heat. Add the onion, garlic, red bell pepper, and jalapeño pepper. Cook for 5-7 minutes or until the vegetables are softened.
2. Add the drained and rinsed black beans to the skillet along with chili powder, ground cumin, salt, and pepper. Cook for another 5 minutes or until the beans are heated through.
3. While the beans are cooking, warm the corn tortillas in a separate skillet or in the oven.
4. To assemble the tacos, place a spoonful of the black bean mixture onto each tortilla. Top with sliced avocado, fresh cilantro, diced tomatoes, and diced red onion.
5. Serve the tacos immediately with lime wedges on the side.

ENCHILADAS

Enchiladas have become such a Tex-Mex classic that it's easy to forget that their origins can be traced back thousands of years. That's when the Aztecs first started dipping corn tortillas in pumpkin seeds, rolling them around hard-boiled eggs, and smothering them in tomato sauce. The fillings have evolved over the years, and chili sauce has become a more common topping (enchilada literally means "in chili"), but the dish's foundation remains the same. That's certainly true with these black bean and sweet potato enchiladas, which should taste both novel and familiar. This festive, colorful dish is sure to be a crowd-pleaser.

PREPARATION TIME
20 MINUTES

COOKING TIME
25 MINUTES

SERVES
4 SERVINGS

INGREDIENTS

For the Enchilada Filling:
- 1 can (15 oz) black beans, drained and rinsed
- 1 cup corn kernels (fresh, frozen, or canned)
- 1 red bell pepper, diced
- 1 small onion, diced
- 2 cloves garlic, minced
- 1 tsp ground cumin
- 1 tsp chili powder
- Salt and pepper, to taste
- 1 tbsp olive oil

For the Enchilada Sauce:
- 2 cups tomato sauce or enchilada sauce
- 1 tsp ground cumin
- 1 tsp chili powder
- Salt and pepper, to taste

For Assembling:
- 8 small corn tortillas
- 1 cup vegan cheese shreds (optional)
- Chopped fresh cilantro, for garnish
- Sliced green onions, for garnish
- Lime wedges, for serving

DIRECTIONS

1. Preheat your oven to 375°F (190°C).
2. Enchilada Filling: In a skillet, heat the olive oil over medium heat. Add the diced onion and red bell pepper. Sauté until the vegetables are softened and slightly caramelized.
3. Stir in the minced garlic, ground cumin, and chili powder. Cook for another minute until fragrant.
4. Add the black beans and corn to the skillet. Season with salt and pepper. Cook for a few minutes until heated through. Remove from heat and set aside.
5. Enchilada Sauce: In a separate bowl, mix together the tomato sauce (or enchilada sauce), ground cumin, and chili powder. Season with salt and pepper to taste.
6. Assembling Enchiladas: Pour a thin layer of the enchilada sauce into the bottom of a baking dish.
7. Warm the corn tortillas by wrapping them in a damp paper towel and microwaving them for about 20-30 seconds. This will make them pliable and easier to roll.
8. Place a spoonful of the enchilada filling onto each tortilla and roll it up. Place the rolled tortillas seam-side down in the baking dish.
9. Pour the remaining enchilada sauce over the rolled tortillas, covering them evenly.
10. Baking: If using vegan cheese, sprinkle the vegan cheese shreds over the enchiladas.
11. Bake the enchiladas in the preheated oven for about 15-20 minutes, or until the sauce is bubbly and the tortillas are slightly crispy around the edges.
12. Serving: Garnish the baked enchiladas with chopped cilantro and sliced green onions.
13. Serve the vegan enchiladas with lime wedges on the side for squeezing over the top.
14. Enjoy your flavorful and satisfying vegan enchiladas!

PAO DE QUEIJO

As I quickly learned in Brazil, pao de queijo (Portuguese for "cheese bread") is a beloved dish. Brazilians pop these bite-sized treats for breakfast or a quick snack. Like many of Brazil's classic dishes, pao de queijo has multicultural roots: the indigenous Guarani tribe began cultivating and pounding cassava to make bread–a tradition that enslaved peoples in Brazil later adopted. Eventually, in the 19th century, cheese was added to the mix, creating the dish we know today. And what a dish it is. It's quick, filling, and completely comforting. And because this recipe uses soy milk for the "cheese," my fellow vegans can enjoy it as well.

PREPARATION TIME
15 MINUTES

COOKING TIME
25 MINUTES

SERVES
16 SERVINGS

INGREDIENTS

- 1 cup unsweetened soy milk
- 1/2 cup vegetable oil
- 2 cups tapioca flour
- 1 tsp salt
- 1/2 tsp garlic powder
- 1/2 tsp onion powder

DIRECTIONS

1. Preheat the oven to 375°F (190°C). Grease a muffin tin with oil or cooking spray.
2. In a blender or food processor, blend the soy milk and vegetable oil until smooth.
3. In a mixing bowl, combine the tapioca flour, salt, garlic powder, and onion powder.
4. Pour the blended soy milk and vegetable oil mixture over the tapioca flour mixture. Stir until well combined and a dough forms.
5. Divide the dough evenly into the greased muffin tin cups, filling each cup about 3/4 full.
6. Bake for 25 minutes or until the pao de queijo is golden brown and puffed up.
7. Remove from the oven and let cool for a few minutes before serving.

FEIJOADA

Brazil is a country with many different regions and cultures. If there is one dish that unifies them all, it's the hearty black bean stew known as feijoada. And in Brazil, there are about as many feijoada recipes as there are households. While I wish I could share them all with you, this basic vegetarian feijoada recipe serves as a great introduction to the dish. Feijoada is typically a festival food meant to be ladled out at large gatherings. So invite some family/friends over and cook up a pot of Brazil's unofficial national dish.

PREPARATION TIME
15 MINUTES

COOKING TIME
1 HOUR 30 MINUTES

SERVES
6 SERVINGS

INGREDIENTS

- 2 cups black beans, soaked overnight and drained
- 2 tbsp olive oil
- 1 onion, chopped
- 3 cloves garlic, minced
- 1 red bell pepper, chopped
- 1 carrot, peeled and chopped
- 1 celery stalk, chopped
- 1 tsp smoked paprika
- 1 tsp ground cumin
- 1 bay leaf
- 2 cups vegetable broth
- 1 cup water
- Salt and pepper to taste
- 1 cup cooked rice (for serving)
- Chopped fresh parsley (for garnish)
- Orange slices (for serving)

DIRECTIONS

1. Start by soaking the black beans overnight. Drain and rinse them before cooking.
2. In a large pot, heat the olive oil over medium heat. Add the chopped onion, minced garlic, red bell pepper, carrot, and celery. Sauté for about 5-7 minutes until the vegetables begin to soften.
3. Stir in the smoked paprika and ground cumin, and cook for an additional 1-2 minutes to release their flavors.
4. Add the soaked and drained black beans to the pot, along with the bay leaf. Pour in the vegetable broth and water.
5. Bring the mixture to a boil, then reduce the heat to low. Cover the pot and let the feijoada simmer for about 1 hour, or until the beans are tender and the flavors are well combined. Stir occasionally and add more water if needed to maintain the desired consistency.
6. During the last 15 minutes of cooking, season the feijoada with salt and pepper to taste.
7. Once the feijoada is cooked and the beans are tender, remove the bay leaf and discard it.
8. Serve the vegetarian feijoada over cooked rice. Garnish with chopped fresh parsley and accompany with orange slices, which are traditionally served with feijoada to enhance the flavors.
9. Enjoy your delicious and hearty vegetarian feijoada!

POTATO PANCAKES

Kartoffelpuffer (potato pancakes) might not be easy to say, but they sure are easy to eat. And they taste even better when eaten in their native Germany, as you can see from this picture of me by Berlin's famous Brandenburg Gate. Potato pancakes are popular across every region of Germany: a savory snack or side that can be seen at restaurants, kitchens, and food stalls across the country. I know some people who like to eat them with ketchup, but for the authentic German way, spread a little applesauce on top. It might sound counterintuitive, but trust me, it's a delightful flavor combination.

PREPARATION TIME
20 MINUTES

COOKING TIME
20 MINUTES

SERVES
4 SERVINGS

INGREDIENTS

- 4 medium russet potatoes, peeled and grated
- 1 small onion, grated
- 2 tbsp all-purpose flour
- 1 tsp baking powder
- 1/2 tsp salt
- 1/4 tsp black pepper
- 2-3 tbsp vegetable oil, for frying
- Applesauce or sour cream, for serving (optional)
- Chopped fresh chives or parsley, for garnish (optional)

DIRECTIONS

1. Preparation: After grating the potatoes and onion, squeeze out any excess moisture using a clean kitchen towel or paper towel. This will help prevent the pancakes from becoming soggy.
2. In a large bowl, combine the grated potatoes and onion.
3. Add the all-purpose flour, baking powder, salt, and black pepper to the bowl. Mix well to combine all the ingredients.
4. Frying: In a large skillet, heat about 2 tablespoons of vegetable oil over medium-high heat.
5. Take spoonfuls of the potato mixture and shape them into patties. Gently press the patties to flatten them slightly.
6. Carefully place the potato patties into the hot skillet. Cook for about 3-4 minutes on each side or until they are golden brown and crispy.
7. As the potato pancakes cook, you may need to add more oil to the skillet to prevent sticking and ensure even frying.
8. Once the potato pancakes are cooked and crispy, remove them from the skillet and place them on a paper towel-lined plate to drain any excess oil.
9. Serving: Serve the vegetarian potato pancakes warm. They can be enjoyed on their own or served with a dollop of applesauce or sour cream. Garnish with chopped fresh chives or parsley if desired.
10. Enjoy your delicious and comforting vegetarian potato pancakes!

APPLE STRUDEL

The Sound of Music will always be one of my favorite musicals. As you may recall, one of the "favorite things" mentioned in the musical's most famous song is "crisp apple strudel." After eating it in Germany, I can see why. If you recall, the musical takes place in Austria, which is where apple strudel hails from. That said, Germans have certainly taken to the gooey dessert, as I saw during my travels there. Naturally, the best apple strudel comes from the best apples, so try to use the freshest you can find, and feel free to mix up varieties for interesting flavor combinations (I like to use Granny Smith and Golden Delicious). It's a rather involved recipe, but the flavor is totally worth it.

100% VEGAN

PREPARATION TIME
30 MINUTES

COOKING TIME
35 MINUTES

SERVES
8 SERVINGS

INGREDIENTS

For the Filling:
- 4 medium apples (such as Granny Smith), peeled, cored, and thinly sliced
- 1/2 cup granulated sugar
- 1 tsp ground cinnamon
- 1/2 tsp ground nutmeg
- 1/2 cup raisins (optional)

- 1/2 cup chopped walnuts or pecans (optional)
- Juice of 1 lemon

For Assembling:
- 8-10 sheets vegan filo pastry, thawed if frozen
- 1/4 cup vegan butter or melted coconut oil
- 1/2 cup breadcrumbs
- Powdered Sugar

DIRECTIONS

1. Preheat your oven to 375°F (190°C). Line a baking sheet with parchment paper.
2. Filling: In a large bowl, combine the sliced apples, granulated sugar, ground cinnamon, ground nutmeg, raisins (if using), chopped nuts (if using), and lemon juice. Toss everything together until the apples are coated with the mixture. Set aside.
3. In a small skillet, melt a small amount of vegan butter or coconut oil. Add the breadcrumbs and toast them lightly until they are golden brown. Remove from heat and set aside.
4. Assembling: Lay a sheet of vegan filo pastry on a clean surface. Brush it lightly with melted vegan butter or coconut oil.
5. Place another sheet of filo pastry on top, slightly overlapping the first sheet. Brush with more melted butter or oil.
6. Repeat the process with 2-3 more sheets of filo pastry, brushing each layer with melted butter or oil.
7. Sprinkle about a tablespoon of toasted breadcrumbs along the long edge of the layered filo pastry. This will help absorb any excess moisture from the apple filling.
8. Filling the Strudel: Spread the apple filling over the breadcrumbs, leaving a border around the edges.
9. Carefully roll the filo pastry and apple filling into a log, tucking in the sides as you go. Place the strudel seam side down on the prepared baking sheet.
10. Brush the top of the strudel with more melted vegan butter or oil.
11. Baking: Bake the apple strudel in the preheated oven for about 30-35 minutes, or until the pastry is golden brown and the apples are tender.
12. Serving: Once the strudel is baked, remove it from the oven and let it cool slightly before slicing.
13. Dust the sliced strudel with powdered sugar.
14. Serve the vegan apple strudel warm, optionally with a dollop of vegan whipped cream or a scoop of vegan vanilla ice cream.
15. Enjoy your delightful and comforting vegan apple strudel!

SAMBAL TOFU

Anyone who knows me knows that I love heat, which is why I am excited to share this next recipe with you. Sambal comes from the Japanese word for "chili paste" and this bright, fiery chili paste can be found all over Southeast Asia, but especially Indonesia. It's often served alongside meals, either for dipping or pouring over noodles or rice. Sambal can either be prepared raw or cooked; this recipe highlights the cooked variety. It's a somewhat time-consuming process, but it will add a deep, spicy flavor to your meals. And a little sambal goes a long way, so feel free to store the remainder in case you need a little heat later on.

PREPARATION TIME
20 MINUTES

COOKING TIME
20 MINUTES

SERVES
4 SERVINGS

INGREDIENTS

For the Sambal Tofu:
- 1 block (14 oz) firm tofu, cubed
- 2 tbsp vegetable oil
- 1 small onion, thinly sliced
- 3 cloves garlic, minced
- 2-3 tbsp vegetarian sambal (or adjust to taste)
- 1 tbsp tamarind paste
- 1 tbsp brown sugar or palm sugar
- Salt to taste
- Chopped cilantro, for garnish

For Serving:
- Cooked rice

DIRECTIONS

1. Preparing the Tofu: Start by draining the tofu and pressing out any excess water. Cut the tofu into cubes.
2. In a skillet or non-stick pan, heat about 1 tbsp of vegetable oil over medium-high heat.
3. Add the tofu cubes to the skillet and cook until they are golden brown on all sides. This will take about 8-10 minutes. Once done, remove the tofu from the skillet and set aside.
4. Making the Sambal Sauce: In the same skillet, heat another tbsp of vegetable oil over medium heat.
5. Add the thinly sliced onion and sauté until it becomes soft and translucent.
6. Stir in the minced garlic and cook for another minute until fragrant.
7. Add the vegetarian sambal to the skillet. The amount can be adjusted based on your preferred level of spiciness.
8. Dissolve the tamarind paste in about 2 tbsp of warm water and add it to the skillet.
9. Stir in the brown sugar or palm sugar and cook the mixture for a few minutes until the flavors meld and the sauce thickens.
10. Combining Tofu and Sambal: Return the cooked tofu cubes to the skillet and gently toss them with the sambal sauce until they are well coated.
11. Season the sambal tofu with salt to taste. Adjust the sweetness and spiciness to your preference by adding more sugar or sambal.
12. Serving: Once the tofu is heated through and coated with the sambal sauce, remove the skillet from the heat.
13. Serve the vegetarian sambal tofu over cooked rice.
14. Garnish with chopped cilantro for added flavor and freshness.
15. Enjoy your delicious and spicy vegetarian sambal tofu!

TOFU SATAY

In my humble opinion, satay is the ultimate street food. Skewered chunks of marinated meat make the perfect snack when you're walking the lush streets of Bali or Jakarta. Since I don't eat meat, I felt left out of the satay party. But now, thanks to this recipe, I can have an Indonesian street snack in my New York apartment whenever I please. This recipe brings fresh island flavors, thanks to ingredients like coconut milk and lime juice, and the creamy peanut sauce is icing on the proverbial cake.

PREPARATION TIME
30 MINUTES

COOKING TIME
15 MINUTES

SERVES
4 SERVINGS

INGREDIENTS

For the Tofu Satay:
- 1 block (14 oz) extra-firm tofu, pressed and cubed
- Wooden skewers, soaked in water

For the Marinade:
- 1/4 cup soy sauce or tamari
- 2 tbsp peanut butter
- 2 tbsp lime juice
- 1 tbsp agave syrup or maple syrup
- 1 tsp curry powder
- 1/2 tsp ground turmeric
- 1/2 tsp ground cumin

- 1/4 tsp ground coriander
- 2 cloves garlic, minced
- 1 tsp grated ginger
- 1/4 tsp red pepper flakes (adjust to taste)
- Salt and pepper, to taste

For the Peanut Sauce:
- 1/4 cup peanut butter
- 2 tbsp coconut milk
- 1 tbsp soy sauce or tamari
- 1 tbsp lime juice
- 1 tbsp agave syrup or maple syrup
- Water, to thin as needed

DIRECTIONS

1. Pressing Tofu: Start by pressing the tofu to remove excess water. Cut the tofu into cubes suitable for skewering.
2. Marinade: In a bowl, whisk together all the marinade ingredients: soy sauce, peanut butter, lime juice, agave syrup, curry powder, turmeric, cumin, coriander, minced garlic, grated ginger, red pepper flakes, salt, and pepper.
3. Add the tofu cubes to the marinade, making sure they are coated evenly. Allow the tofu to marinate for at least 30 minutes or longer if time allows. You can marinate in the refrigerator.
4. Skewering: While the tofu is marinating, soak the wooden skewers in water. This prevents them from burning while cooking. Once the tofu is marinated, thread the tofu cubes onto the skewers.
5. Grilling/Baking: You can either grill the skewers on a barbecue or cook them in the oven. If grilling, preheat the grill to medium-high heat. If baking, preheat the oven to 375°F (190°C). Grill or bake the skewers for about 12-15 minutes, turning occasionally, until the tofu is cooked and has grill marks or is slightly browned.
6. Peanut Sauce: While the tofu skewers are cooking, prepare the peanut sauce. In a small bowl, whisk together the peanut butter, coconut milk, soy sauce, lime juice, and agave syrup. Add a little water to thin the sauce to your desired consistency.
7. Serving: Once the tofu skewers are cooked, remove them from the grill or oven.
8. Serve the tofu satay skewers with the peanut sauce for dipping.
9. Garnish with chopped fresh cilantro and crushed peanuts.
10. Enjoy your flavorful and protein-rich vegan tofu satay!

SHEPARD'S PIE

Shepherd's pie is easily one of the United Kingdom/Ireland's most famous culinary exports, up there with fish & chips and bangers & mash. This hearty dish provides all the warmth and sustenance one needs for a cold winter in the U.K. Turns out, it's pretty helpful for those cold American winters, too. While shepherd's pie usually features lamb or beef, this vegetarian version substitutes mushrooms for meat. And, yes, it still goes perfectly with a frothy pint of Guinness!

PREPARATION TIME
20 MINUTES

COOKING TIME
30 MINUTES

SERVES
6 SERVINGS

INGREDIENTS

For the Filling:
- 2 cups cooked lentils (green or brown)
- 1 cup diced carrots
- 1 cup frozen peas
- 1 onion, diced
- 2 cloves garlic, minced
- 1 cup vegetable broth
- 1 tbsp tomato paste
- 1 tsp dried thyme
- 1 tsp dried rosemary
- Salt and pepper, to taste

For the Mashed Potato Topping:
- 4-5 large potatoes, peeled and diced
- 1/4 cup vegan butter or margarine
- 1/4 cup plant-based milk (such as almond or oat milk)
- Salt and pepper, to taste

For Assembling:
- 1/2 cup shredded vegan cheese (optional)

DIRECTIONS

1. Mashed Potatoes: Start by boiling the diced potatoes in a pot of salted water until they are tender. Drain the potatoes and return them to the pot.
2. Mash the potatoes using a potato masher or fork. Add the vegan butter or margarine and plant-based milk. Continue to mash until the potatoes are smooth and creamy. Season with salt and pepper to taste. Set aside.
3. Filling: In a large skillet, heat a little oil over medium heat. Add the diced onion and cook until it becomes translucent.
4. Add the minced garlic, diced carrots, and frozen peas to the skillet. Sauté for a few minutes until the vegetables start to soften.
5. Stir in the cooked lentils, tomato paste, dried thyme, and dried rosemary. Cook for another couple of minutes, allowing the flavors to meld.
6. Pour in the vegetable broth and bring the mixture to a simmer. Let it cook for about 5-7 minutes until the liquid has reduced and the filling has thickened. Season with salt and pepper to taste.
7. Assembling the Pie: Preheat your oven to 400°F (200°C).
8. Transfer the lentil and vegetable filling to a baking dish. Spread it out evenly.
9. Spoon the mashed potato mixture over the filling, using a fork to create a decorative pattern on top. You can also sprinkle shredded vegan cheese over the mashed potatoes if desired.
10. Baking: Place the baking dish in the preheated oven and bake for about 15-20 minutes, or until the top is golden brown and the filling is bubbly.
11. Serving: Once the shepherd's pie is cooked, remove it from the oven.
12. Garnish with chopped fresh parsley if desired.
13. Serve the vegetarian shepherd's pie warm, and enjoy this hearty and comforting dish!

BAILEY'S CHEESECAKE

I honestly can't decide which I like more: a splash of Bailey's or a rich cheesecake. You might as well enjoy both! Did you know that cheesecake has been around - in some form - since the 5th century BCE? That's when the ancient Greeks started mixing fresh cheese with flour and honey and cooking them on an earthenware griddle. Bailey's Irish Cream is much younger than that: it was created by London advertising exec Tom Jago. For many, though, it captures the flavors and spirit of Ireland. And when baked into a cheesecake, it makes a beloved dessert even better.

PREPARATION TIME
30 MINUTES

COOKING TIME
50 MINUTES (PLUS CHILLING TIME)

SERVES
8-10 SERVINGS

INGREDIENTS

For the Crust:
- 1 1/2 cups vegan graham cracker crumbs (or crushed vegan cookies)
- 1/4 cup melted coconut oil or vegan butter
- 2 tbsp granulated sugar

For the Filling:
- 2 cups raw cashews, soaked for at least 4 hours or overnight
- 3/4 cup Bailey's Almande (vegan Bailey's alternative)
- 1/2 cup coconut cream
- 1/2 cup maple syrup or agave syrup

- 1/4 cup melted coconut oil
- 1 tsp vanilla extract
- Zest of 1 lemon
- Pinch of salt

For the Chocolate Ganache:
- 1/2 cup vegan chocolate chips
- 1/4 cup coconut cream
- 2 tbsp Bailey's Almande

For Topping:
- Vegan whipped cream
- Chocolate shavings or cocoa powder

DIRECTIONS

1. Preparing the Crust: In a bowl, combine the vegan graham cracker crumbs, melted coconut oil or vegan butter, and granulated sugar. Mix until the crumbs are well coated.
2. Press the crumb mixture into the bottom of a greased 9-inch springform pan, creating an even layer. Place the pan in the freezer while you prepare the filling.
3. Preparing the Filling: Drain and rinse the soaked cashews. In a high-speed blender, combine the soaked cashews, Bailey's Almande, coconut cream, maple syrup, melted coconut oil, vanilla extract, lemon zest, and a pinch of salt. Blend until the mixture is smooth and creamy.
4. Pour the filling over the prepared crust in the springform pan. Smooth the top with a spatula.
5. Baking the Cheesecake: Place the cheesecake in the refrigerator and let it chill for at least 4 hours or until it is set.
6. Preparing the Chocolate Ganache: In a small saucepan, heat the coconut cream until it is hot but not boiling. Remove from heat and stir in the vegan chocolate chips until they are fully melted, and the mixture is smooth. Add Bailey's Almande and mix well.
7. Allow the chocolate ganache to cool slightly before pouring it over the chilled cheesecake. Use a spatula to spread the ganache evenly over the top.
8. Chilling the Cheesecake: Return the cheesecake to the refrigerator and let it chill for an additional 1-2 hours or until the ganache is set.
9. Serving: Before serving, carefully remove the sides of the springform pan. Top the cheesecake with vegan whipped cream and chocolate shavings or cocoa powder.
10. Slice and serve your delicious vegan Bailey's cheesecake!

KIMCHI FRIED RICE

To say that kimchi is a Korean staple is an understatement: this piquant dish of fermented vegetables (often cabbage) is eaten with nearly every meal, and it's been that way for thousands of years. And while it's often eaten as a side, this fried rice recipe puts kimchi front-and-center. Homemade kimchi yields the best flavors for this dish, but that process can take a couple of weeks. If you're raring to get started on this recipe ASAP, head to your local specialty store and pick up a jar of kimchi. I won't blame you one bit.

100% VEGAN

PREPARATION TIME
10 MINUTES

COOKING TIME
20 MINUTES

SERVES
2 SERVINGS

INGREDIENTS

- 1 cup white rice
- 2 cups kimchi, coarsely chopped
- 1 cup kimchi juice
- 1 small onion, diced
- 2 cloves garlic, minced
- 1/4 cup kale
- 2 tbsp vegetable oil
- 1 egg
- Spring onion to garnish
- 1 tbsp of black sesame to garnish (optional)

DIRECTIONS

1. In a large saucepan of 3 cups water, cook rice according to package instructions; set aside.
2. Heat oil in a pan over medium-high heat. Add garlic and onion, stirring frequently, until onions have become translucent, about 2-3 minutes.
3. Add kimchi to the pan and cook until golden.
4. Stir in rice, kale and kimchi juice mixture until the kale has wilted, about 2-3 minutes.
5. Serve topped with a fried egg. Sprinkle finely-sliced spring onion and black sesame to garnish.

KOREAN RICE CAKES

Chuseok (also known as Hangawi) is a three-day harvest festival celebrated every mid-autumn in South Korea. Like all the best festivals, Chuseok has a robust menu. One of the festival favorites is Songpyeon: stuffed rice cakes. These colorful, half-moon-shaped rice cakes are stuffed with a sweet filling of sugar, honey, and sesame seeds. And while they are a definite fall treat, I won't fault you for making some in the winter. Or spring, or summer, for that matter.

PREPARATION TIME
15 MINUTES

COOKING TIME
20 MINUTES

SERVES
4 SERVINGS

INGREDIENTS

- 1 package (16 oz) vegetarian rice cakes (cylinder-shaped or flat)
- 1/2 cup vegetarian kimchi, chopped
- 1/2 cup sliced carrots
- 1/2 cup sliced bell peppers (any color)
- 1/2 cup sliced onion
- 2 cloves garlic, minced

- 3 tbsp gochujang (Korean red pepper paste)
- 2 tbsp soy sauce or tamari
- 1 tbsp sugar
- 1 tsp sesame oil
- 4 cups vegetable broth
- 1 tbsp vegetable oil
- Toasted sesame seeds and chopped green onions, for garnish

DIRECTIONS

1. Preparing the Rice Cakes: If using frozen rice cakes, thaw them according to the package instructions. If using dried rice cakes, soak them in warm water for about 10-15 minutes until they soften. Drain and set aside.
2. Sautéing Vegetables: In a large skillet or pan, heat the vegetable oil over medium heat. Add the minced garlic and sauté for a minute until fragrant.
3. Add the sliced carrots, bell peppers, and onion to the skillet. Sauté for about 3-4 minutes until the vegetables start to soften.
4. Creating the Sauce: In a bowl, mix together the gochujang (Korean red pepper paste), soy sauce, sugar, and sesame oil to create the sauce.
5. Cooking Vegetables and Rice Cakes: Add the chopped kimchi to the skillet and sauté for another minute.
6. Pour in the vegetable broth and the prepared sauce. Stir well to combine the ingredients and bring the mixture to a gentle simmer.
7. Add the vegetarian rice cakes to the skillet. Let them simmer in the sauce for about 10-15 minutes until they are heated through and have absorbed some of the sauce.
8. Adjusting the Sauce: Taste the mixture and adjust the seasoning if needed. You can add more gochujang for extra heat, more sugar for sweetness, or more soy sauce for saltiness.
9. Serving: Once the rice cakes are tender and coated with the sauce, remove the skillet from the heat.
10. Serve the vegetarian Korean rice cakes hot, garnished with toasted sesame seeds and chopped green onions.
11. Enjoy this savory and flavorful dish as a main course or snack!

MILK TEA

Is milk tea the new latte? It's certainly having its moment in the U.S., with milk tea shops popping up on seemingly every street corner. The drink originated in Hong Kong but was transformed in the 1980s when Taiwanese tea merchants started adding tapioca balls (boba) to the mix. Bubble tea was born, and it quickly swept the U.S., thanks in large part to the Taiwanese community in Southern California. This recipe is just for milk tea sans boba. You can buy boba pretty easily these days, and it's surprisingly simple to make. Perhaps a recipe for my next cookbook...

PREPARATION TIME
5 MINUTES

COOKING TIME
10 MINUTES

SERVES
2 SERVINGS

INGREDIENTS

- 2 black tea bags (or tea of your choice)
- 2 cups boiling water
- 1 cup plant-based milk (such as almond, soy, oat, or coconut milk)
- 2-3 tbsp sweetener (such as agave syrup, maple syrup, or cane sugar)
- 1/2 tsp vanilla extract (optional)
- Ice cubes (optional)

DIRECTIONS

1. Brewing the Tea: Start by placing the black tea bags in a teapot or heatproof pitcher. Pour the boiling water over the tea bags and allow them to steep for about 3-5 minutes, or until the tea reaches your desired strength.
2. Removing Tea Bags: Once the tea has steeped, remove the tea bags from the teapot.
3. Adding Sweetener: While the tea is still hot, stir in the sweetener of your choice. Adjust the amount to achieve your preferred level of sweetness.
4. Adding Plant-Based Milk: Allow the tea to cool slightly before adding the plant-based milk. Stir in the plant-based milk until well combined.
5. Adding Vanilla Extract (Optional): If desired, you can add a touch of vanilla extract to enhance the flavor of the milk tea.
6. Chilling the Milk Tea: If you prefer your milk tea cold, you can refrigerate it for a while or add ice cubes to it.
7. Serving: Pour the vegan milk tea into glasses filled with ice cubes (if using). Serve the milk tea immediately and enjoy!

DUMPLINGS

One of the things I've learned from my global culinary adventures is that nearly every culture has some form of beloved dumpling, whether that be American chicken & dumplings, Polish pierogies, Italian ravioli, Japanese gyoza, or these delicious vegan dumplings that I fell in love with in China. These savory cabbage, mushroom, and spinach dumplings will be the perfect addition to your next dim sum party. And if you don't have one scheduled, get on that ASAP. I may have some additional recipes for you.

PREPARATION TIME
40 MINUTES

COOKING TIME
15 MINUTES

SERVES
40 SERVINGS

INGREDIENTS

FILLING:
- 1 medium cabbage roughly 3.5lbs, you can also use napa cabbage
- 1 bunch of spinach replace with bok choy
- 2 tofu skin finely chopped. You can also use: dry tofu or extra firm tofu crumbled and fry until golden
- 15 dried shiitake mushrooms soak for 20 mins in warm water before use (or until soft)
- 3 small bunches of cellophane noodles (mung bean noodles). Soak for 20 mins in warm water before use (or until soft)
- 2 skinny carrot finely chopped

SEASONING:
- 5 tbsp soy sauce
- 4 tbsp sesame oil
- 1 tbsp sugar
- 1 tbsp freshly grated ginger
- 2 tsp ground white pepper
- 1 tsp salt or to taste

DUMPLING WRAPPERS:
- 1-1/2 Portion of homemade dumpling wrapper

DIRECTIONS

1. Bring a medium pot of water to boil.
2. While the water is heating, clean and chop the cabbage into 8 wedges, spinach into 2" pieces so it's easier to blanch.
3. Add the cabbage to the pot of boiling water to blanch for 10 seconds, spinach for 5 seconds. Drain and let cool. The reason the veggie has to be blanched ahead is to control how much water there is in the dumplings. By blanching the veg, it's softened, and excess water can be squeezed out later.
4. While waiting for the veggies to cool, chop the tofu skin, soaked mushrooms (squeeze the juice out), and cellophane noodles into roughly 5mm pieces. Carrots need to be chopped slightly finer than that. Mix all the chopped ingredients in a large mixing bowl.
5. Once the blanched veggies are cool enough to handle, chop them up into 5mm pieces, then move to a nut milk bag/ laundry bag and squeeze out about 80% of the water. That's abstract, I know. I usually squeeze mine with both hands until the veggies clump together and form a ball without falling apart easily and not too soggy to touch.
6. Add the squeezed veggies to the mixing bowl and mix in the seasoning: 5 tbsp soy sauce, 4 tbsp sesame oil, 1 tbsp sugar, 1 tbsp freshly grated ginger, 2 tsp ground white pepper, and 1 tsp salt (or to taste). Mix well. The best part about making vegan dumplings is that you can taste them and adjust accordingly!
7. Finally, it is ready for dumpling wrapping.

ACKNOWLEDGMENTS

Now it's time for my favorite part of the book: giving a shout-out to everyone whose support made it all possible. I have a lot of amazing people in my life, and I wouldn't be anywhere close to where I am today without them.

It starts with my family, who took me into their homes and loved me unconditionally (I'm sure it wasn't always easy). Mom, my love of cooking comes from you, and I can only hope my dishes make you proud. Dad, you encouraged my natural curiosity about the world. I promise to never stop exploring it. And to my brother Naveen, faithful taste tester of some of my earliest recipes (sorry!), I rely on your insightful feedback to this day. I know you're going to take the natural skincare industry by storm. And, of course, I can't forget my furry friend and constant companion, Zelda. Thanks for always being a joy to come home to, even if you tried almost every recipe in this cookbook while my back was turned.

I also want to thank my birth parents, who made the hard decision to give me up for adoption. Although I've never met you, I have cherished the opportunity to explore the roots that you gave me. And thanks to all my friends - both here and abroad - who have shared their stories and culinary wisdom with me. My favorite part of traveling will always be the people I am privileged to meet.

I want to give a big shout-out to everyone who has inspired my cooking and travels. It would take me at least another book to mention everyone, but I will try to restrain myself. Vegan chefs like Amanda Cohen and Isa Chandra Moskowitz have redefined plant-based cooking in America. I would be honored to one day join your ranks. Travel-wise, I must mention the late, great Anthony Bourdain, whose shows I never missed (even with my hectic chef's schedule). Thank you for showing me how to explore the world as a student and not a tourist.

While researching this book, I read about as many cookbooks as I could get my hands on (shout out to the New York Public Library!). Some - like a great novel - I couldn't put down. Specifically, I loved Between Harlem and Heaven by JJ Johnson and Alexander Smalls; On Vegetables by Jeremy Fox; Salt, Fat, Acid, Heat by Samin Nosrat; and - last but certainly not least, Mastering the Art of French Cooking by my girl Julia Child. Reading these books improved my cooking and writing, and I can't recommend them enough.

Huge props to everyone who helped put this book - and my site - together: Brandon Ross, Tori Ross, Toni Aston, Brandon Wuske, Rofelyn Yap, Clarice Jamilano, Alejandro Corona, Carolina Sosa, and Yiit Ayyıldız. If there is anyone I am forgetting, please let me know–I'll make you dinner.

Finally, thank you to all of my loyal readers (yes, that includes you!). It's been a pleasure sharing my journey with you.

Thanks for coming along for the ride!

COMMON KITCHEN SWAPS

As a vegan chef, one of the questions I get asked most often is, "How do I make my favorite dish vegetarian or vegan?" Short answer: it's all about the substitutes. And you would be shocked at how many people wind up not missing meat or dairy at all, once they've found the right ingredients to swap out. Whether you're craving pork, beef, chicken, seafood, butter, or cheese (the hardest thing for me to give up at first), you can find something that imitates the flavor and texture of your favorite animal product. Here is a quick cheat sheet for swapping out vegetarian/vegan ingredients:

> **Meat**   →   Jackfruit, tofu, tempeh, or legumes

> **Eggs**   →   Flaxseed or chia seed

> **Cream**   →   Coconut cream

> **Honey**   →   Maple syrup or agave nectar

> **Gelatin**   →   Agar agar

> **Chicken or Beef Broth**   →   Vegetable broth

> **Cheese**   →   Plant-based cheese or nutritional yeast

> **Butter**   →   Vegan butter, coconut oil, or olive oil

> **Milk**   →   Almond milk, rice milk, or coconut milk

CHEF JADE, SIGNING OFF

Thank you for joining me on my whirlwind culinary adventure. We've covered 56 recipes from over a dozen countries and cooked everything from feijoada to milk tea, to good old pancakes. I don't know about you, but I could use a nap...and maybe some takeout.

This cookbook - like my life - has been quite the journey. Writing this cookbook has allowed me to more deeply explore and connect with my diverse heritage while doing what I love most: cooking. Actually, scratch that; cooking comes in at a close second. The thing I love most is sharing my recipes, experiences, and whatever insights I've gleaned along the way with you, my readers.

I've tried to accommodate as many tastes and cultures as I could within the spectrum of vegan/vegetarian cooking. I know that every recipe in a cookbook this large isn't going to be the perfect fit for every cook, but I hope that you've found at least a few solid recipes to add to your repertoire. And I hope you get to share them with the people in your life. That, after all, is the true joy of cooking. I'm sorry if I'm starting to sound like a Hallmark card, but come on, it's my first cookbook! I'd be remiss not to get a little sentimental.

Actually, a lot sentimental. This wouldn't have been possible without you, and I am so grateful for your support. I also couldn't have done it without the many people (and one cheeky dog) whom I have met along the way– starting with my family, who were brave (foolish?) enough to let me loose in the kitchen at an early age. Sorry for all the near house fires–I hope I've done you proud. I also need to give a shout out to the strangers-turned-family who were gracious enough to share their favorite dishes and preparations with me, whether that be grandmas in Greece or street vendors in Rio.

But I still have a lot to learn and even more to cook. Enough to fill up another cookbook, most likely. I hope you will continue to accompany me and Zelda on our journey, wherever it takes us. Now, if you'll excuse me, I have to pack my bags. London's calling.

INDEX

INDEX

INDEX

INDEX

INDEX

INDEX

INDEX

INDEX

INDEX

INDEX

INDEX

Made in the USA
Middletown, DE
18 November 2024

64393852R00071